RSC

Swan Theatre

HYDE PARK
by James Shirley

A programme/text with commentary by Simon Trussler

Contents

Swan Theatre Plays published by Methuen London
by arrangement with the Royal Shakespeare Company

RSC
Swan Theatre

The Royal Shakespeare Company (RSC), is the title under which the Royal Shakespeare Theatre, Stratford-upon-Avon, has operated since 1961. Now one of the best-known theatre companies in the world, the RSC builds on a long and distinguished history of theatre in Stratford-upon-Avon.

In essence, the aim of the Company is the same as that expressed in 1905 by Sir Frank Benson, then director of the Stratford theatre: 'to train a company, every member of which would be an essential part of a homogenous whole, consecrated to the practice of the dramatic arts and especially to the representation of the plays of Shakespeare'. The RSC is formed around a core of associate artists – actors, directors, designers and others – with the aim that their different skills should combine, over the years, to produce a distinctive approach to theatre, both classical and modern.

When, just a year after the granting, in 1925, of its Royal Charter, the theatre was almost completely destroyed by fire, a worldwide campaign was launched to build a new one. Productions moved to a local cinema until the new theatre, designed by Elisabeth Scott, was opened by the Prince of Wales on 23 April, 1932. Over the next thirty years, under the influence of directors such as Robert Atkins, Bridges-Adams, Iden Payne, Komisarjevsky, Sir Barry Jackson, Glen Byam Shaw and Anthony Quayle, the Shakespeare Memorial Theatre maintained a worldwide reputation.

In 1960, the newly appointed artistic director, Peter Hall, extended the re-named Royal Shakespeare Company's operations to include a London base at the Aldwych Theatre, and widened the Company's repertoire to include modern as well as classical work. Other innovations of the period which have shaped today's Company were the travelling Theatregoround and experimental work which included the Theatre of Cruelty season.

Under Trevor Nunn, who took over as artistic director in 1968, this experimental work in small performance spaces led, in 1974, to the opening of The Other Place, Stratford-upon-Avon. This was a rehearsal space converted into a theatre and in 1977 its London counterpart, The Warehouse, opened with a policy of presenting new British plays. In the same year the RSC played its first season in Newcastle upon Tyne – now an annual event. In 1978, the year in which Terry Hands joined Trevor Nunn as artistic director, the RSC also fulfilled an ambition to tour towns and villages with little or no access to live professional theatre.

In 1982, the RSC moved its London base to the Barbican Centre in the City of London, opening both the Barbican Theatre, specially built for the RSC by the generosity of the Corporation of the City of London, and The Pit, a small theatre converted like The Warehouse and The Other Place, from a rehearsal room.

Last season saw the opening of this new RSC theatre: the Swan. Built within the section of the shell of the original Shakespeare Memorial Theatre which escaped the 1926 fire, the Swan is a Jacobean-style playhouse staging the once hugely popular but now rarely-seen plays of Shakespeare's contemporaries during the period 1570-1750. This new dimension to the Royal Shakespeare Company's work has been made possible by the extremely generous gift of Frederick R. Koch, the RSC's benefactor. The Swan, too, now has its London counterpart. In March 1987 the RSC moved into the Mermaid Theatre, the Barbican's City neighbour. There it will perform the Swan repertoire and three new productions in a year-round season, presented by Frank and Woji Gero and Playhouse Productions Ltd. In early 1987 Terry Hands became sole Artistic Director and Chief Executive of the Company.

Throughout its history, the RSC has augmented its central operations with national and international tours, films, television programmes, commercial transfers and fringe activities. It has won over 200 national and international awards in its 25 years, including most recently the Queen's Award for Export – but despite box office figures which, it is thought, have no equal anywhere in the world, the costs of RSC activities cannot be recouped from ticket sales alone. We rely on assistance from the Arts Council of Great Britain, amounting to about 40% of our costs in any one year, from work in other media and, increasingly, from commercial sponsorship. To find out more about the RSC's activities and to make sure of priority booking for our productions, why not become a member of the Company's Mailing List. Details of how to apply can be found in the theatre foyer.

CAST IN ORDER OF APPEARANCE

Trier	**James Fleet**
Lacy	**Richard McCabe**
Venture	**Paul Spence**
Jarvis	**Bill McGuirk**
Lord Bonvile	**John Carlisle**
Lord Bonvile's Page	**David Pullan**
Rider	**Sean Pertwee**
Mistress Bonavent	**Pippa Guard**
Mistress Carol	**Fiona Shaw**
Fairfield	**Alex Jennings**
Master Bonavent	**Paul Webster**
Julietta	**Felicity Dean**
A Waiting Woman	**Kate Littlewood**
Jockey	**Laban Leake**
Stable Lad	**Jeremy Gilley**
Milkmaid	**Jane Whittenshaw**
Wedding Guests	**Kate Littlewood**
	Jane Whittenshaw
	Jeremy Gilley
	Laban Leake
Runners	**Jeremy Gilley**
	Laban Leake

Other parts are played by members of the company.

MUSICIANS

piano	**John Woolf**
flute	**Ian Reynolds**
clarinet	**Edward Watson**
trumpet/cornet	**Brian Allen**
cello	**Alan Carus-Wilson**
percussion	**Clifford Pick**
Directed by	**Barry Kyle**
Designed by	**Gerard Howland**
Lighting by	**Wayne Dowdeswell**
Music by	**Jeremy Sams**
Movement by	**Sheila Falconer**
Sound by	**Paul Slocombe**
Music Director	**John Woolf**
Assistant Director	**Nicholas Mahon**
Company voice work by	**RSC Voice Department**
Stage Manager	**Rachael Whitteridge**
Deputy Stage Manager	**Alastair John-Duncan**
Assistant Stage Manager	**Susan Dale**

'At the age of eight the young Virginia Woolf edited her first publication, a newspaper for family and friends. It was called the "Hyde Park Gate News".'

First performance of this RSC production: Swan Theatre, Stratford-upon-Avon, 7 April 1987.

Arts Council Funded

Biographies

JOHN CARLISLE *Lord Bonvile*
Theatre: Seasons at Harrogate, Ipswich, Birmingham, Liverpool. The Common Man in *A Man For All Seasons*, Gary Essendine in *Present Laughter*, Billy in *Billy Liar*, Mick in *The Caretaker*, Henry Carr in *Travesties*, Astrov in *Uncle Vanya* (Repertory). ADC to Skorkorsky in *Soldier*, Harold in *The Boys in the Band*, Cassius in *Julius Caesar*, Jacques in *As You Like It*, Lunatic/Political Prisoner in *Every Good Boy Deserves Favour* (London), *Relatively Speaking*, *Conduct Unbecoming* (UK tours), directed and played Harold in *The Boys in the Band* (Dublin).
RSC: The King in *The Maid's Tragedy*, Apemantus in *Timon of Athens*, Parson in *The Fool*, Ulysses in *Troilus and Cressida*, Pastor/Devil in *Peer Gynt*, Gremio in *The Taming of the Shrew*, Rector in *The Body*, Don Juan in *Much Ado About Nothing* (also Europe and USA), Minister in *Softcops*, King in *Molière*, Edward IV in *Richard III*, Canterbury/Burgundy in *Henry V*, Boyet in *Love's Labour's Lost*, Ralph Nickleby in *Nicholas Nickleby*.
Television: *Emergency Ward 10*, *The Haggard Falcon*, *New Scotland Yard*, *Time Lock*, *It's Good to See You*. *The Rivals of Sherlock Holmes*, *Hadleigh*, *Rules, Rules, Rules*, *Thirty Minute Theatre*, *The Tay Bridge*, *Kidnapped*, *Disraeli*, *The Omega Factor*, *Cyrano de Bergerac*, *Molière*.

FELICITY DEAN *Julietta*
Theatre: *Rookery Nook* (Taunton), *The Schoolmistress* (Royal Exchange Manchester), *Hayfever* (Lyric, Hammersmith), *Much Ado About Nothing* (Oxford Playhouse tour), *Pericles* (Theatre Royal Stratford East), Ginny in *Relatively Speaking* (Greenwich Theatre), Olivia in *Twelfth Night* (Leicester Haymarket), *An Honourable Trade* (Royal Court).
RSC: *Good* (London and New York).
Television includes *Short Back and Sides*, *Play for Today – Shooting the Chandelier*, *Who's Who*, *The Birds Fall Down*, *The Legend of King Arthur*, *The Happy Autumn Fields*, *Play for Today – The Trouble with Gregory*, *The Member for Chelsea*, *The Far Pavilions*, *Play of the Month – The Blue Dress*.
Films: *Return to Munich*, *Success is the Best Revenge*, *Steaming*, *Water*, *Revolution*, *Whistle Blower*.

WAYNE DOWDESWELL *Lighting*
Theatre: *The Fantasticks*, *Salad Days*, Verdi's *Macbeth*, *Nabuco* and *Aida*, Mozart's *Cosi Fan Tutte*, *Don Giovanni* (Sheffield University Theatre), *No More Sitting On the Old School Bench*, *Painted Veg and Parkinson*, *Fanshen*, *The Hunchback of Notre Dame* (Manchester Contact Theatre).
RSC: Joined the RSC in 1978. Worked at TOP as Deputy Chief Electrician and Chief Electrician. TOP productions include *Money*, *Golden Girls*, *Desert Air*, *Today*, *The Dillen*, *Mary After the Queen*, *The Quest*. Currently Resident Lighting Designer at the Swan Theatre where his productions include *The Two Noble Kinsmen*, *Every Man in His Humour*, *The Rover* and *The Fair Maid of the West*.

SHEILA FALCONER *Movement*
RSC: Includes *As You Like It*, *The Relapse*, *Toad of Toad Hall*, *The Winter's Tale*.
Opera: *The Italian Girl in Algiers* (Opera 80), *Faust* (Opera North), *Faust*, *Cavalleria Rusticana/I Pagliacci*, *The Merry Widow* (English National Opera), *Ruddigore* (NSWO), *Ariodante* (Buxton Festival). Many musicals including *Merrily We Roll Along* (Bloomsbury Theatre).
Film: *Lady Jane*.

JAMES FLEET *Trier*
Theatre: Seasons at Perth, Pitlochry. Romeo in *Romeo and Juliet*, Jimmy Porter in *Look Back in Anger*, Marchbanks in *Candida*, Simon in *Mary Rose* (Repertory). Kiri Kuki in *The Crimson Island*, Ian in *One Orange for the Baby*, Garth Esdras in *Winterset* (Gate Theatre).
RSC: Flute in *A Midsummer Night's Dream*, Somerton in *The Witch of Edmonton*, Subtleman in *The Twin Rivals*, Slightly in *Peter Pan*, Peregrine in *Volpone*, Willie Faroughly in *The Time of Your Life*, Joshua Farr in *The Dillen*, Walter Kent in *Waste*.
Television: *Grange Hill*, *The Omega Factor*, *Dempsey and Makepeace*.
Films: *Defence of the Realm*, *Crazy Like a Fox*.

JEREMY GILLEY *Jockey*
Theatre: Title role in *Bugsy Malone* (Her Majesty's).
Television: *Alas Smith and Jones*, *Paradise Postponed*, *Punch Drunk*. To be released – *Succubus*.

PIPPA GUARD *Mistress Bonavent*
Theatre: Faye in *A Chorus of Disapproval* (National Theatre and Lyric, Shaftesbury Avenue), title role in *Antigone* (National Theatre).
RSC: Hermia in *A Midsummer Night's Dream*, Luciana in *The Comedy of Errors*, Evie in *Factory Birds*.
Television: *The Mill on the Floss*, *The Tempest*, *All's Well That Ends Well*, *A Midsummer Night's Dream*, *To the Lighthouse*, *The Flipside of Dominic Hyde*, *The Country Diary of an Edwardian Lady*, *The Life and Loves of a She Devil*.
Film: *An Unsuitable Job for a Woman*.

GERARD HOWLAND *Designer*
Theatre: Commenced career as Head of Design at Marlowe Theatre, Canterbury. Then moved to West Germany as Head of Design for Dortmund's four theatres where productions included *Uncle Vanya*, *The Father*, *Andorra*, *Arms and the Man*, *Accidental Death of an Anarchist*.
RSC: *The Winter's Tale*, *Scenes From a Marriage*.
Opera: includes *Jenufa*, *Madam Butterfly*, *La Traviata*, *La Bohème*, *Orpheus in the Underworld* (West Germany), *Cavalleria Rusticana* and *I Pagliacci* (English National Opera), *Ariodante* (Buxton Festival0).

ALEX JENNINGS *Fairfield*
Seasons at Bristol Old Vic, York, Leeds, Southampton, Manchester Royal Exchange, Chichester. Mr Sparkish in *The Country Wife*, Sir Andrew Aguecheek/Orsino in *Twelfth Night*, the Clown in *Antony and Cleopatra*, Luigi in *Can't Pay? Won't Pay*, Algernon in *The Importance of Being Earnest*, Simon Bliss in *Hay Fever*, title role in *Macbeth* (Repertory). Lt Hargreaves in *For King and Country* (Greenwich), The Groom in *A Respectable Wedding* (King's Head), Robespierre in *The Scarlet Pimpernel* (Her Majesty's), Mr Darbey in *Dandy Dick* (Cambridge Theatre Company tour),
Television: *Smiley's People*, *The Kit Curran Show*.
Radio: Extensive work on BBC Radio.

BARRY KYLE *Director*
Theatre: *The Merchant of Venice* (Tel Aviv), *The Maid's Tragedy* (Melbourne).
RSC: Associate Director of the RSC. Co-directed *Cymbeline*, *King John*. Directed *Sylvia Plath*, *Comrades*, *Perkin Warbeck*, *Richard II*, *Dingo*, *That Good Between Us*, *Troilus and Cressida*, *Frozen Assets*, *Measure for Measure*, *The Churchill Play*, *The White Guard*, *Julius Caesar*, *Sore Throats*, *The Irish Play*, *The Maid's Tragedy*, *Thirteenth Night*, *The Witch of Edmonton*, *Bond's Lear*, *The Taming of the Shrew*, *The Roaring Girl*, *The Dillen*, *Mary After the Queen*, *Golden Girls*, *The Crucible*, *Love's Labour Lost*, *The Two Noble Kinsmen*, *Richard II*.

LABAN LEAKE *Jockey*
Theatre: Squire Jason in *Beauty and the Beast*, The Dog in *Tinder Box* (Globe Children's Theatre), Old Bill in *Lunch Break* (Bubble Theatre).

KATE LITTLEWOOD *A Waiting Woman*
Theatre: Lucy in *She Also Dances* (Offstage Downstairs), Nola in *All You Deserve* (Cockpit), Lily in *The King and the Corpse* (Almeida), Temba Theatre Company tour.
Television: *You Meet All Sorts*.
RSC: Translated *Worlds Apart* by José Triana (TOP 1986).

NICHOLAS MAHON *Assistant Director*
Studied drama at University of East Anglia. Plays directed there included *The Homecoming* and *The Seagull*. Worked as an assistant director at Glasgow Citizens' Theatre on *A Woman of No Importance* and *She Stoops to Conquer* amongst others. Recently directed *The Promise* at the Latchmere Theatre for One Word Theatre Company.
RSC: Assistant Director on *The Danton Affair*, *Much Ado About Nothing*, *The Merchant of Venice*, *Scenes From a Marriage*, *Hyde Park*. Director – *The Guest Room* (Not the RSC Festival).

RICHARD McCABE *Lacy*
Theatre: Seasons at Sheffield Crucible, Bolton, Manchester Royal Exchange. *Renaissance*, *The Alchemist*, *The Changeling* (Sheffield Crucible), Mozart in *Amadeus* (Bolton), Simon in *Hay Fever*, Touchstone in *As You Like It* (Manchester Royal Exchange), *Pistols* (Theatre Royal, Plymouth), Mercutio in *Romeo and Juliet* (Leeds Playhouse), *Should Auld Acquaintance* (Bolton Octagon). *Some of My Best Friends Are Husbands* (Leicester Haymarket UK tour), *As You Like It* (Royal Exchange, Manchester tour).
RSC: Bentley Summerhays in *Misalliance*.
Television: *The Bill*, *Bullman*.
Other: played, toured and recorded with two bands, *The Spectres* and *Tenpole Tudor*.

BILL McGUIRK *Jarvis*
Theatre: The Caretaker in *Don't Just Lie There Say Something*, The Captain in *The Heretic*, Doctor in *Snap*, Reverend Garison in *Wildfire* (London). Inspector McIvor/Dr Angelus in *Dr Angelus*, Inspector Wilson in *Not in the Book*, Colonel Melody in *A Touch of the Poet*, (UK tours), *Further Confessions of a Window Cleaner* (tour to Zimbabwe).
RSC: Little Murders, Cinna the Conspirator in *Julius Caesar*, Jack Rugby in *The Merry Wives of Windsor*, The Shoemaker in *The Relapse*, *The Indians*.
Television: *Z Cars*, *Softly Softly*, *The Professionals*, *Coronation Street*, *The Old Man at the Zoo*, *Death of a Young Young Man*, *Strike*.
Films: *The Straw Dogs*, *The Persuaders*.
Opera: Baron Grog in *The Grand Duchess of Gerolstein* (Sadlers Wells).

SEAN PERTWEE *Rider*
Theatre: Seasons at Swan Theatre Worcester. Damis in *Tartuffe*, Ernest/Phylis Fontain in *Once in a Lifetime*, Policeman/Franky Perkins in *Blood Brothers*, Doormouse/Gryphon/Knave of Hearts in *Adventures of Alice* (Repertory). Follywit in *It's a Mad World My Masters* (Bristol), Nipper in *Class Enemy*, Myrmidon in *Demon Barber* (Bristol), Dogberry in *Much Ado About Nothing* (Bristol), Dudley in *Breaking the Ice* (Swansea). *The Nativity*, *Cowardy Custard*, *Intergalactic Noah*, *Plugg* (UK tours).
Television: *Frontline*, *A Mugger*.
Films: *Prick Up Your Ears*.
Radio: *The Long, the Short and the Tall*, *An Inspector Calls*.

DAVID PULLAN *Page to Lord Bonvile*
Theatre: Title role in *Macbeth*, Sir Gawain in *Sir Gawain and the Green Knight* (The Acting Co, Australia), Elias in *Dickinson*, Nick in *Roses in Due Season* (Troupe Company Australia), Ned Hawkins in *The Ballad of Billy Lane* (Shaw Theatre), *A Midsummer Night's Dream* (Schools tour).
RSC: Sir James Blunt in *Richard III* (Australian tour).
Television: *Round and Round*, *Moving*, *Central Week*, *Mussolini*, *For the Term of His Natural Life*.
Films: *Maurice*, *Dirty Dozen III*, *The Trumpet is a Liar*.

JEREMY SAMS *Composer*
Theatre: Composer and Musical Director for *Ring Round the Moon*. *Jumpers* (Royal Exchange, Manchester), *Vanity Fair* (Cheek by Jowl), *The Blue Angel* (Liverpool Playhouse), *On the Razzle* (Leeds Playhouse). *The Scarlet Pmpernel* (Chichester, West End), *As You Like It* (Royal Exchange), *The Merchant of Venice* (British Council tour), Musical Director for *Carousel* (Royal Exchange), *Carmen Jones* (Sheffield Crucible).
RSC: *The Merry Wives of Windsor, Crimes in Hot Countries, Downchild, The Castle, A Midsummer Night's Dream*. Musical Director for *The Winter's Tale, The Crucible* (RSC/Nat West tour).
Radio: Talks and recitals on Radio 3.
Writing: Opera translations: *Johnny Strikes up* (Opera North), *Zemire et Azor* (Camden Festival).

FIONA SHAW *Mistress Carol*
Theatre: Rosaline in *Love's Labour's Lost* (Bolton), Mary Shelley in *Bloody Poetry* (Leicester and Hampstead), Julia in *The Rivals* (NT).
RSC: Tatyana Vasilyevna in *Philistines*, Celia in *As You Like It*, Madame de Volanges in *Les Liaisons Dangereuses*, Erika Brückner in *Mephisto*. Beatrice in *Much Ado About Nothing*, Portia in *The Merchant of Venice*.
Television: *Fireworks for Elspeth, Sherlock Holmes, Love Song, Sacred Hearts*.

PAUL SPENCE *Venture*
RSC: Newsboy/Sailor in *The Time of Your Life*, Alworth in *A New Way to Pay Old Debts*, Castrone in *Volpone*, Yagoda in *Red Star*, Lord in *Twelfth Night*, the Young Man in *Mother Courage*, Nibs in *Peter Pan*, Fenton in *The Merry Wives of Windsor*, Jacques de Boys in *As You Like It*, Helenus in *Troilus and Cressida*, Hans Miklas in *Mephisto*, Hérault de Séchelles in *The Danton Affair*, James Giddy in *A Penny For a Song*.

PAUL WEBSTER *Master Bonavent*
Theatre: Includes seasons at Liverpool, Manchester and Birmingham. Title roles in *Hamlet, Richard II, Richard III, Macbeth*, Sir Thomas More in *A Man for All Seasons*, title role in *Othello* (Repertory), Resident co-director and actor at the Library Theatre, Manchester, 1967-74.
RSC: Gremio in *The Taming of the Shrew*, Colonel Ball in *The Churchill Play*, Ephraim Smooth in *Wild Oats*, Adolphus Grigson in *The Shadow of a Gunman*, Vosmibratov in *The Forest*, Warrington in Bond's *Lear* (UK and European tour), Lepidus in *Antony and Cleopatra*, Alonso in *The Tempest*, Dr Brink in *The Custom of the Country*, Reverend Paris in *The Crucible*, Antigonus in *The Winter's Tale* (UK tour and Poland), George Page in The Merry Wives of Windsor, The Dillen, Gratiano in *Othello*, Josthinkel in *Mephisto*, Antonio in *The Merchant of Venice*, Leonato in *Much Ado About Nothing*.
Broadcasting: over thirty years of broadcasting in plays, documentaries and poetry readings.

JANE WHITTENSHAW *Milkmaid*
Theatre: Seasons at Leeds Playhouse, Belgrade Coventry, Young Vic. *Passion Play, Romeo and Juliet, Blood Brothers. What a Way to Run a Revolution* (Young Vic), *Merrily We Roll Along* (Bloomsbury Theatre). *Papertown Paperchase* (Whirligig Theatre Co UK tour).
RSC: *Nicholas Nickleby* (UK and US tour 1985/6).
Television: *South Bank Show – Stephen Sondheim Masterclass, Let's Pretend, What a Way to Run a Revolution*.

JOHN WOOLF *Music Director*
RSC: Music Director for *Cymbeline, Julius Caesar* (1979), *Othello* (1979), *Romeo and Juliet, King Lear, The Roaring Girl, Julius Caesar* (1983), *Twelfth Night, The Comedy of Errors, Philistines, Troilus and Cressida, The Winter's Tale, A Midsummer Night's Dream*. Arranged music for *The Twin Rivals* and *Molière*.

UNDERSTUDIES

Jeremy Gilley *Rider/Trier*
Laban Leake *Lacy/Venture*
Kate Littlewood *Julietta/Mistress Bonavent*
Bill McGuirk *Master Bonavent*
Sean Pertwee *Lord Bonvile/Jarvis*
Jane Whittenshaw *Waiting Woman/Mistress Carol*

Royal Shakespeare Company

Stratford-upon-Avon Box Office (0789) 295623

ROYAL SHAKESPEARE THEATRE

Julius Caesar
by William Shakespeare
directed by Terry Hands

The Merchant of Venice
by William Shakespeare
directed by Bill Alexander

Twelfth Night
by William Shakespeare
directed by Bill Alexander

The Taming of the Shrew
by William Shakespeare
directed by Jonathan Miller

Measure for Measure
by William Shakespeare
directed by Nicholas Hytner

SWAN THEATRE

Hyde Park
by James Shirley
directed by Barry Kyle

Titus Andronicus
by William Shakespeare
directed by Deborah Warner

The Jew of Malta
by Christopher Marlowe
directed by Barry Kyle

The Revenger's Tragedy
by Cyril Tourneur
directed by Di Trevis

The New Inn
by Ben Jonson, directed by John Caird

THE OTHER PLACE

Fashion
by Doug Lucie
directed by Nick Hamm
by arrangement with Michael Codron

Temptation
by Vaclav Havel trans. by George Theiner
directed by Roger Michell

Indigo
by Heidi Thomas
directed by Sarah Pia Anderson

A Question of Geography
by John Berger and Nella Bielski
directed by John Caird

Cymbeline
by William Shakespeare
directed by Bill Alexander

London Box Office (01) 628 8795

BARBICAN THEATRE

Macbeth
by William Shakespeare
directed by Adrian Noble

Romeo and Juliet
by William Shakespeare
directed by Michael Bogdanov

Richard II
by William Shakespeare
directed by Barry Kyle

THE PIT

Country Dancing
by Nigel Williams
directed by Bill Alexander

Worlds Apart
by Jose Triana, adapted by Peter Whelan
directed by Nick Hamm

Sarcophagus
by Vladimir Gubaryev
Translated by Michael Glenny
directed by Jude Kelly

MERMAID THEATRE

The Fair Maid Of The West
by Thomas Heywood
directed by Trevor Nunn

Every Man In His Humour
by Ben Jonson
directed by John Caird

The Two Noble Kinsmen
by William Shakespeare and John Fletcher
directed by Barry Kyle

RSC in the West End

PALACE THEATRE
Box Office (01) 437 6834/8327
Les Miserables
The Victor Hugo musical

AMBASSADORS THEATRE
Box Office (01) 836 6111
Les Liaisons Dangereuses
by Christopher Hampton

THE OLD VIC
Box Office (01) 928 7616
Kiss Me Kate
Cole Porter's musical from 8 May

Swan Theatre

Royal Shakespeare Company

Incorporated under Royal Charter as the
Royal Shakespeare Theatre
Patron Her Majesty the Queen
President Sir Kenneth Cork
Chairman of the Council Geoffrey A Cass
Vice Chairman Dennis L Flower
Artistic Director Terry Hands
Direction Peggy Ashcroft John Barton Peter Brook
Terry Hands Trevor Nunn

Technical Services Administrator John Bradley
General Manager David Brierley
Publicity Controller Peter Harlock
Production Controller James Langley
Planning Controller Tim Leggatt
Senior Administrator Genista McIntosh
Barbican Administrator James Sargant
Financial Controller William Wilkinson

Deputies
Finance David Fletcher
Planning Carol Malcolmson
Production Simon Opie

Heads of Department

Cicely Berry *Voice*
Siobhan Bracke *Casting*
Colin Chambers *Literary*
Andy Clark *Data Processing*
Brian Davenhill *Scenic Workshop*
Tony Hill *Education*
Jane Jacomb-Hood *Sponsorship*
Brenda Leedham *Wigs and Make-up*
John A Leonard *Sound*
William Lockwood *Property Shop*
Nigel Loomes *Paint Shop*
Viviana Maranzano *Merchandising*
Peter Pullinger *Construction*
Frances Roe *Wardrobe*
John Watts *Safety*
Guy Woolfenden *Music*

Swan Theatre

Judith Cheston *Press* (0789) 296655
Sonja Dosanjh *Company Manager*
Wayne Dowdeswell *Chief Electrician*
Brian Glover *RSC Collection*
Josie Horton *Deputy Wardrobe Mistress*
Barry Kyle *Artistic Director*
Geoff Locker *Production Manager*
Philip Medcraft *Master Carpenter*
Janet Morrow *Publicity*
Chris Neale *House Manager*
Richard Power *Deputy Chief Electrician*
Eileen Relph *House Manager*
Richard Rhodes *Deputy Theatre Manager*
Graham Sawyer *Theatre Manager*
Ursula Selbiger *Box Office Manager*
Michael Tubbs *Music Director*

Production Credits for Hyde Park

Costumes from Cosprop, London. Additional costumes made in
RST Workshops, Stratford-upon-Avon. Stagecloth made by
Frederick Freer, Warwick. With thanks to Peter and Frankie
Conner for devising the tic-tac. Swan Property Manager Mark
Graham. RSC programme compiled by Sue Skempton. Production photographs by Michael Le Poer Trench.

Facilities

In addition to bar and coffee facilities on the ground floor, there is
wine on sale on the first floor bridge outside Gallery 1. Toilets,
including facilities for disabled people, are situated on the
ground floor only.

RSC Collection

Over a thousand items on view: costumes, props, pictures and
sound recordings illustrating the changes in staging from
medieval times to the use of the thrust stage in the Swan, and
comparisons of past productions of the current season's plays.
Come and see our exhibition; browse in the sales and refreshments area – and book a backstage tour. Open weekdays from
9.15am, Sundays from 12.00.

The Two Noble Kinsmen, Swan Theatre 1986

The Fair Maid of the West, Swan Theatre 1986

Hugh Quarshie: ARCITE

Gerard Murphy: PALAMON

Pete Postlethwaite: ROUGHMAN,
Imelda Staunton: BESS BRIDGES

Brian Lawson: EXECUTIONER
Sean Bean: SPENCER

Every Man in His Humour, Swan Theatre 1986

The Rover, Swan Theatre 1986

Nathaniel Parker: WELLBRED,
Simon Russell Beale: ED KNO'WELL

Pete Postlethwaite: CAPTAIN BOBADILL,
Paul Greenwood: MASTER STEPHEN,
Roger Moss: CLEMENT'S SERVANT,
Simon Russell Beale: ED KNO-WELL

Geraldine Fitzgerald: FLORINDA, Jenni George: CALLIS,
Hilary Townley: VALERIA

Jeremy Irons: WILMORE, Hugh Quarshie: BELVILE

Stage History

The Master of the Revels issued his licence for *Hyde Park* on 20 April 1632, and it is likely that it was first performed shortly afterwards by Christopher Beeston's company, Queen Henrietta's Men, at their Phoenix Theatre (sometimes called the Cockpit), a 'private' or indoor playhouse, the first to be situated in Drury Lane. No cast list has survived, but from what we know of the players with Queen Henrietta's Men around this time, and of their specialities, one might guess that if the reputedly dashing John Sumner took the role of Fairfield, then the company's other leading men, the protean Richard Perkins and Michael Bowyer, would have had equal claims upon Lacy and Trier. William Sherlock, who specialized in the more swaggering sorts of villain, might have been best suited for Lord Bonvile, while the relatively 'heavy' Anthony Turner would have found Bonavent closest to his taste in a play which is unusual in its lack of the elderly authority-figures for which he was noted.

Hyde Park was evidently still popular in 1639, when it was included in a list of plays acknowledged to be the property of the King and Queen's Young Company, better known as Beeston's Boys, by then in occupation at the Phoenix. We know that it was revived at least once during the Restoration, when Pepys in his diary records going on 11 July 1668 to 'the King's playhouse' – that is, the first Theatre Royal in Drury Lane, off Bridges Street – to see 'an old play of Shirley's, called *Hyde Park*, the first day acted'. Although he noted that 'horses are brought on the stage', Pepys found it 'a very moderate play, only an excellent epilogue spoke by Beck Marshall'. This production evidently played before royalty on 14 July, but there is no record of subsequent performances or revivals in the professional London theatre.

Synopsis

Lacy is paying suit to Mistress Bonavent, whose husband has bound her to wait seven years for his return before presuming him lost at sea. Meanwhile her cousin, Mistress Carol, rejects all three of her suitors, playing off Rider and Venture against one another, and spurning Fairfield. Fairfield's sister Julietta appears to reciprocate the love of Lacy's friend Trier but is angered when he tests her affections by telling the amorous Lord Bonvile that she is a whore, and leaves her to his noble friend's pursuit. The intrigues and deceptions continue amidst the social and sporting occasions of Hyde Park.

Commentary
by Simon Trussler

James Shirley: a Brief Chronology

1596 7 Sept., baptised in parish church of St. Mary Woolchurch (on site of the present Mansion House), eldest son of James Sharlie of London.

1608 4 Oct., began attending Merchant Taylors' School, off Upper Thames Street. Left in 1612?

1613-15 Apprenticed to the scrivener Thomas Frith?

1615 Matriculated, and entered St. Catherine's College, Cambridge, as a pensioner in Easter term.

1617 Awarded his BA Degree and left Cambridge.

1618 Publication of his narrative poem, *Echo and Narcissus*. 1 June, married Elizabeth Gilmet of St. Albans, where he had become Master of the Grammar School. At uncertain dates between now and 1625 he was ordained into the church, was subsequently converted to Roman Catholicism, and was back in London for the baptism of his eldest son Mathias on 26 Feb. 1625.

1625 Beginning of his twelve-year relationship, probably contractual, with Christopher Beeston's company at the Phoenix, playing as Lady Elizabeth's Men when his first extant play, the comedy *Love Tricks; or, The School of Compliment* was performed (published 1631). The company was reformed as Queen Henrietta's following the accession of Charles I.

1626 *The Maid's Revenge*, described as his second tragedy (published 1639) – the first presumably being the lost *Tragedy of St. Albans*. The comedy *The Wedding* (published 1629) probably also performed this year, by Queen Henrietta's Men at the Phoenix (where they continued to play until 1636).

1628 The comedy *The Witty Fair One* (published 1633) performed by Queen's Men.

1629 The tragi-comedy *The Grateful Servant* (published 1630) performed by Queen's Men.

1631 The tragedy *The Traitor* (published 1635), the romance *The Duke; or, The Humorous Courtier* (published 1640), and the tragedy *Love's Cruelty* (published 1640), all performed by Queen's Men.

1632 The comedy *The Changes* (published 1632) probably presented at Salisbury Court theatre by Prince Charles's.

company. The comedies *Hyde Park* (published 1637) and *The Ball* (published 1639) performed by Queen's Men. Earliest likely date for the romance adapted from Sidney, *The Arcadia* (published 1640).

1633   The romantic comedy *The Bird in a Cage* (published 1633), the comedy *The Gamester* (performed at court, and published 1637), and the tragi-comedy *The Young Admiral* (published 1637), performed by Queen's Men. Publication of the short moral masque *A Contention for Honour and Riches* (probably unacted, but expanded in 1658).

1634   Admitted to membership of Gray's Inn, the records describing him as 'one of the valets of the chamber of Queen Henrietta Maria'. His masque *The Triumph of Peace* (published 1634) performed at court under the auspices of the Inns of Court. The comedies *The Example* (published 1637) and *The Opportunity* (published 1640) performed by Queen's Men. Revised Fletcher's *The Night-Walker*.

1635   The romantic comedy *The Coronation* (published 1640) and the comedy *The Lady of Pleasure* (published 1637) performed by Queen's Men. Revision of Chapman's *Chabot, Admiral of France* (published 1639).

1636   The tragi-comedy *The Duke's Mistress* (published 1638), last of his plays to be performed by Queen Henrietta's Men. 12 May, all London theatres closed until the autumn of 1637 by prolonged outbreak of plague. Shirley left for Dublin, probably in Nov. 1636, remaining there until 1640.

1637   For John Ogilby's newly-built Werbergh Street theatre Shirley wrote the Irish historical drama *St. Patrick for Ireland* (published 1640) and the romantic comedy *The Royal Master* (published 1638), the latter also performed by the second Queen's Men, playing at Salisbury Court in 1638.

1638   The comedy *The Constant Maid* (published 1640) and the tragi-comedy *The Doubtful Heir* (published 1653) probably first performed in Dublin, the latter also staged in London by the King's Men in 1640..

1639   The tragi-comedy *The Gentlemen of Venice* (published 1655) and the tragedy *The Politician* (published 1655) probably first performed in Dublin, then by second Queen's Men in London.

1640   Returned to London following the death of Massinger in March, and became dramatist for the King's Men, playing at the Blackfriars and the Globe, beginning with the tragi-comedy *The Imposture* (published 1653) and the comedy *The Country Captain* (written with William Cavendish, Earl of Newcastle, and published in 1649).

1641   The comedy *The Brothers* (published 1653) and the tragedy *The Cardinal* (published 1653) both performed by King's Men.

1642   The comedy *The Sisters* (published 1653) performed by King's Men, and the tragi-comedy *The Court Secret* (published 1653) written for them, but unperformed owing to the closure of the theatres upon the outbreak of civil war in September.

1644   May have joined the Earl of Newcastle's forces on the king's side in the Civil Wars, but soon believed to have returned to London and lived quietly and fairly prosperously as a schoolmaster.

1646   Published a collection of his *Poems*, mainly non-dramatic verse, but also including the masque *The Triumph of Beauty*.

1647   Assisted in the publication of the folio collection of plays ascribed to Beaumont and Fletcher, contributing an address to the reader.

1653   *Six New Plays* (those written for the King's Men) published. The masque *Cupid and Death* presented before the Portuguese ambassador, and also published.

1658   The moral allegory *Honoria and Mammon* (expanded from *A Contention for Honour and Riches*, 1633) and the entertainment *The Contention of Ajax and Ulysses* both published, but not known to have been acted.

1666   Died, with his second wife Frances (date of marriage unknown), apparently after a miserable flight from the Great Fire of London. 29 Oct., buried at St. Giles in the Fields. His will discloses a relatively large estate, and names three sons, two daughters and their husbands, and a grandson.

The Theatre of Caroline London

The dramatic career of James Shirley fits with a neatness that is almost disconcerting into the Caroline period. He wrote his first plays in 1625, the year in which Charles I came to the throne, while his last work for the professional stage came in 1642, when the theatres were closed on the outbreak of civil war. An earlier closure had occurred in 1625, when the period of mourning for the old King James overlapped with a particularly virulent outbreak of the plague; and the canny theatre manager Christopher Beeston seized this opportunity to 'break' his old company, in order to secure the patronage of Charles's newly-wed French wife for a new grouping. Shirley's happy transformation from schoolmaster to playwright coincided with the formation of this new company, for whom he served as regular dramatist, or 'ordinary poet', until 1636. Known as Queen Henrietta's Men, the troupe performed at Beeston's Phoenix Theatre, and soon became chief rivals to London's longest surviving company, the King's Men. The chief writer for the King's Men, John Fletcher – who followed Shakespeare in that capacity – had been carried off by the plague, and when his successor Philip Massinger died in 1640, it was James Shirley who was chosen to replace him. In between, he had been serving as 'ordinary poet' for the first permanent playhouse in Dublin, and thus spent his entire theatrical life in a close working relationship with a major professional company.

The Phoenix Theatre had been converted from a cockpit in 1616, and was a 'private' or indoor house – as was the Blackfriars, the winter home of the King's Men, where they had become the first adult company to act under cover in 1609. A little to the west of the Blackfriars, between Fleet Street and the Thames, a third roofed theatre, the Salisbury Court, was built in 1629, originally for a short-lived company of adult and boy players known as the King's Revels. Another company, generally known as the second Prince Charles's (to distinguish them from the group which had played under Charles's patronage as heir apparent), also performed there before a further outbreak of plague closed all the theatres for fifteen months in 1636-37 – upon which the opportunistic Beeston dissolved Queen Henrietta's Men, and put a new troupe called the King and Queen's Young Company (or more simply Beeston's Boys) into the Phoenix, while a new group of Queen Henrietta's Men went to Salisbury Court. The second Prince Charles's then played at the Red Bull and Fortune Theatres, beyond the northern boundary of the City of London, and seems to have shared these venues with an obscure troupe known as the Red Bull-King's Men.

The Red Bull was London's oldest theatre still in regular use, having been converted from the original inn around 1604, while the Fortune had been rebuilt on the site of the earlier house of that name in 1623. Both were 'public' or outdoor theatres – to whose number must, of course, be added the Globe on Bankside, rebuilt in 1613 and still the home of the King's Men during the summer months. So London could still boast three open-air theatres which catered for the wider, popular audience unable to afford the prices at the private houses – also three in number, but considerably smaller in their capacities. Since the public theatres relied heavily on revivals from the Elizabethan and Jacobean repertoires, their continuing significance in the Caroline period has often been underestimated. In truth, there had been no sudden break with the earlier theatrical tradition on which they drew: simply, the better-off among their audiences had gradually drifted to the private theatres, for which the new plays, more distinctively 'Caroline' in sensibility, were largely written.

The 'third theatre' of Caroline London was that of the court – but just as the King's Men took their Blackfriars repertoire to the Globe in the summer, so also were they prominent among those commanded to present plays before the king, generally at the Cockpit-in-Court in Whitehall. In the early sixteen-thirties, Queen Henrietta's Men were second only to the King's in contributing to the twenty or so plays presented there each year – in addition, that is, to the masques staged exclusively at court, lavish entertainments of which Ben Jonson wrote the better-known earlier examples, and in which his old sparring-partner Inigo Jones continued to be involved till the end came with the politically-charged *Salmacida Spolia* in 1640. Professional dramatists continued to provide their services as masque-writers, and Shirley's own *The Triumph of Peace* was staged at Shrovetide 1634 under the auspices of the Inns of Court. But, under Henrietta Maria's influence, several courtiers also tried their hands at playwriting, besides participating in the action – as did the queen herself in *The Shepherd's Paradise*, for which the author, Walter Montague, second son of the Earl of Manchester, reputedly received the astounding sum of £2,500.

Whether or not one is persuaded by Martin Butler's contention that even the 'courtier plays' acted on occasion as 'an important focus and voice for anxieties and dissent existing in tension with the court', it must be acknowledged that the audience reached by the masques, however influential, was relatively small. To assume, as many authorities have done, that the 'tone' of Caroline drama was set by the dilettante dramatics of a 'cavalier court' is to make quite unwarranted assumptions about the influence exerted by that court over the 'fashionable' audiences at the private playhouses – and is virtually to ignore the continuing strength of the popular tradition at the public theatres.

Playgoing: Privileged or Popular?

Writers of 'survey histories' of theatre almost always leapfrog from the Elizabethan (under which they tend to subsume the Jacobean) into the accommodating lap of the Restoration. If Caroline theatre gets a mention – beyond the small matter of its demise in 1642 – it is for an alleged 'decadence', which is duly attributed to its increasing dependence on courtly patronage. The forging of such untimely links with the 'cavalier camp', it is suggested, not only compromised the future of the theatre as an institution, but also cut it off from the 'popular' audiences which had nourished the drama of Shakespeare's day. This was before the publication of *The Privileged Playgoers of Shakespeare's London,* in which Ann Jennalie Cook set out to demonstrate that even Elizabeth audiences were drawn largely from a social elite, fluid though its composition may have been. So there never *was* a popular audience?

Historians such as Lawrence Stone have helped us to understand that the political crisis of the mid-seventeenth century was due not to increased assertiveness on the part of the aristocracy, but to its actual decline in relation to the nobility and the gentry. The theatre historian Martin Butler has further shown that if we take proper care to distinguish between these social classes, rather than assuming them all to be vaguely 'courtly', we can arrive at a far better understanding not only of the composition of Caroline theatre audiences, but of the distinctive qualities of the plays they saw. Simply, there was no real equivalent in the London of the sixteen-thirties to the exclusive 'beau monde' of the Restoration, intimately associated as it was with the small circle surrounding the king. At a time before the nobility and landed gentry felt the need or wish to leave the business of their country estates for more than a month or two at most in London – and in a decade when Charles's attempt at personal rule prevented members of parliament from combining business with metropolitan pleasures – the composition of 'the town' was constantly changing, and in no clear way separate in its sense of values from 'the country'.

As Butler succinctly puts it: 'in Jacobean city comedies, country wealth is a prey for the rapacity of the city, while in Restoration versions the gaiety of town life destroys any sympathy for the values of the country' – but this 'mutually destructive aspect' is absent from most plays of the Caroline period. The focus shifts geographically, from 'the city' of Jacobean drama to 'the town' – from the business life of the square mile, to the leisured activities of the West End, around the Strand and the newly laid-out Covent Garden – but there is also a recognition that the London thus identified is essentially a meeting-place. The theatre in general, and the work of professional dramatists such as Shirley in particular, was thus doing more than passively reflecting a society which, as Butler puts it, was still 'defining its own internal boundaries': it was offering 'models for its behaviour'.

It's also important to remember that the decade or so before the civil war was rather less 'overcast by its shadow' than retrospective tradition glibly suggests. Such parliaments as Charles permitted to meet were constantly looking *back* rather than forwards, generally reminding themselves and the king of his inferiority to Elizabeth, now virtually a cult-figure. Strong divisions of opinion there certainly were, but, as Butler forcefully argues, these were as much raw material for 'two-sided debate by the theatre and among its audience' as within 'the new social milieu' itself. And Butler demonstrates that this milieu embraced people with 'strong provincial ties or from a commercial background' – forces which were excluded from (or at best despised by) the more restrictive world of Restoration society, as of its theatre. Until very late indeed, almost all the forces which opposed the behaviour of the king did *not* question the authority of his office as constitutionally defined: they were aiming at reformation, not revolution. And even when military conflict erupted, the order for the closure of the theatres in September 1642 was almost certainly not intended to be more permanent than earlier closures on account of royal deaths, or, all too frequently, the plague, but simply as a normal precaution against public disorder. In the event, it was to remain in force for eighteen years.

New plays which drew upon the concerns and uncertainties of the shifting and highly amorphous elite of Caroline London naturally found their way into the private theatres which provided that elite with the creature comforts it expected. Old plays, often reflecting the glories (or at least the supposedly less complicated values) of the Elizabethan world, met the same kinds of uncertainties and concerns as they affected the popular audiences at the public theatres. Not the least valuable aspect of Butler's work is its almost casual demolition of Cook's belief in Shakespeare's 'privileged playgoers' – but in the final analysis, as Butler himself says, 'the most powerful rebuttal of Cook's assertions lies in the character of the plays themselves'. Although the last half-dozen plays written by James Shirley before the outbreak of civil war catered to the tastes of their intended first audiences at the Blackfriars, even they were written in the knowledge that they must satisfy also the far larger summer audiences at the Globe. If that's decadence, its appeal was of a kind that most modern theatre companies would envy.

Professionalism and the 'Ordinary Poet'

Some of the major playwrights of the Elizabethan and Jacobean period – notably Jonson, Chapman, Middleton, and Webster – worked largely as free-lances, and had no permanent relationship with any single theatre company. But James Shirley followed the example of such earlier writers as Heywood, Fletcher, Dekker, Massinger, and of course Shakespeare, in the almost continuous association he maintained with an acting troupe. So too did his close contemporary, Jonson's friend and disciple Richard Brome, whose contract with the new company of Queen Henrietta's Men which played at Salisbury Court after the plague closure of 1736-37 is the only extant example of such an agreement. It has survived because it became the subject of a law suit, in which the company alleged that Brome had broken the clauses in his contract guaranteeing his exclusive service and the number of plays he was to provide each year.

The evidence of Shirley's career suggests that he probably worked under similar conditions to Brome. Thus, G. E. Bentley points out that Shirley's regular work for Queen Henrietta's Men from 1625 to 1636, and subsequently for the King's Men from 1640 to 1642, reveals a markedly similar pattern – 22 plays in eleven years for his first company, six plays in three for his last. He seems to have provided, in short, a 'spring' and an 'autumn play' annually for each troupe, though plague closures and other incidents mean that the pattern is not precisely reflected in dates of first performances. Shirley wrote for another company during these years only on the occasion of *The Changes* being staged at Salisbury Court, probably early in 1632 – and the play's prologue and epilogue both refer to this shift in allegiance. Bentley offers the interesting suggestion that this may have marked the period between the expiration of Shirley's first seven-year contract with Queen Henrietta's Men and the negotiation of a new – to which process a tentative spreading of his wings might have been calculated to add impetus.

Brome's contract also prohibited him from publishing any of his plays without his company's consent – as almost certainly did Shirley's. Thus, only five of Shirley's 22 plays for Queen Henrietta's Men were published while he was still writing for them, evidently with their approval – but no less than thirteen further plays from that period went into print between 1637 and 1640, once the relationship had ended. And *none* of the six plays Shirley wrote for the King's Men between 1640 and 1642 was published during that time, only reaching print in a collected volume of 1653 – by which time, as Bentley puts it, 'eleven years of suppression had killed all hope for a revival of the old days'. Although 'courtier plays' in particular seem to have circulated more widely in manuscript than would have been likely in Shakespeare's time, companies were evidently still trying to protect their ownership of plays by limiting their publication – and we may conjecture that it is only Shirley's initial change of allegiance, and subsequently the closure of the theatres, that ensured so high a proportion of his work coming down to us in print.

Apart from its interest in reflecting the relationship between theatre companies and their 'ordinary poets', the pattern of Shirley's work suggests a pragmatic and professional attitude towards his craft which is far removed from the dilettante dabbling of the courtier writers. If Shirley's plays belong to a 'decadence' – that easy pejorative cast like a pall over the period by so many critics – then the moral deterioration implied by the term must have to do with the content of the plays and their supposed social attitude, not with any slackness in the author's commitment to his craft. In reading the plays, however, one is struck by the direct relationship between their dramatic energy and their concern with the immediacies of Caroline society – the traditionally derided 'comedies of manners' surpassingly more alive in this respect than the tragedies once said to contain Shirley's 'most memorable work'. Certainly, of Shirley's half-dozen or so tragedies, only the last – *The Cardinal* (1641), with its Websterian echoes – is undeserving of the faint damnation once lavished by Edmund Gosse as intended praise: 'There is here an agreeable absence of violence, a recurrence of honest and wholesome fancies and reflections, and a vein of poetry that is genuine if not very deep or rich.' Well, yes.

Tragi-comedy, merging imperceptibly into romance, was, of course, more to the taste of the times, and with the exception of a handful of masques – and that wayward product of his Dublin years, the historical sport *St Patrick for Ireland* – the remainder of Shirley's output was split more or less equally between comedies of London life and these fashionable package tours of the Italian courts, abounding with disguised or substituted lovers, interludes of low comedy, and rightful heirs climactically restored. It is tempting to wax psychological about the needs such plays satisfied for their audiences, and they do indeed deal largely in the triumphant reassertion of traditional values. But if – despite Martin Butler's ingenious suggestion that *The Duke's Mistress* (1636) satirises the platonic idealism of Queen Henrietta's circle – the tragi-comedies scarcely question the accepted order of things, the interest of the comedies springs in part from their dealing with a London society whose very uncertainty about the 'accepted order' contributes to their creative tension.

Comedies of Contrasting Manners

Shirley's comedies of manners are almost all set in London – and almost all contrast the values of 'the town' with those of 'the court' on the one hand and those of 'the country' on the other. At his best, Shirley presents this opposition dramatically, not schematically – and he also displays a Jonsonian delight in the incidental nonsenses of life which healthily inhibits any tendency to moralise. One such incidental nonsense was evidently the preferred ingredient in his first extant play, *Love Tricks* (1625), to judge by its publication under its original sub-title, *The School of Compliment* – a reference to the almost detachable middle act in which, for a fee, fashionable affectations are taught to the uninitiated. In *The Wedding* (1626), too, a main plot self-consciously reminiscent of *Much Ado* is redeemed by the comic density of its details of daily life, as also by its happily intrusive sub-plot. In this, two contrasting cowards muddle their way to a duel – at a time, it's worth noting, when would-be men of fashion were no more confident about the proper etiquette of duelling than they were about other 'rules' of social behaviour. In *The Witty Fair One* (1628) the leading characters are, sure enough, fresh from the country, where the traditional values of courtesy, hospitality, and independence are still taken for granted. Such values are contrasted with the futile aspirations of an upstart knight, whom, significantly, we first meet being *instructed* in his behaviour – in this case, in the new, foreign fashions which are supplanting sturdy native manners. The leavening of the absurd is here provided by the antics of the rakish Fowler, whose spiralling despair when all his acquaintances decide to behave as if he were dead makes his last-act reformation rather less psychologically perfunctory than usual.

In the four years which elapsed before his next group of London comedies, Shirley gained considerably in dramatic assurance. Placing less reliance on mechanically-contrived plots, he allowed himself a refreshingly discursive approach – even giving the plagiaristic Caperwit time to discourse in *The Changes* (1732) upon the poetic function of the adjective. The changes themselves are rung upon the possible couplings of no less than three pairs of lovers, while the foolish knight Sir Gervase Simple – who has himself been wooing a page disguised as a rich widow – achieves wisdom only in his eventual decision to 'turn yeoman in the country again'. *Hyde Park* was Shirley's spring offering for Queen Henrietta's Men in 1632, and was followed in the autumn by *The Ball* – which, like *Hyde Park*, was less concerned with plot than with the local colour suggested by its title. Conceived in emulation of the French salon, the ball was an invention of this decade – originating, significantly, in the need of those without a large house in town to hire a more suitable West End setting in which to entertain their acquaintances. The ballroom no less than the theatre quickly became a convenient place for meeting, match-making, and gossip – and both, as Martin Butler points out, were venues independent of the court. Shirley's portrayals in *The Ball* of those pioneering the new fashion were evidently accurate, since the Master of the Revels required him to excise passages thought to caricature living originals.

Conventional amorous intrigues are to the fore again in *The Gamester* (1633), and the venerable bed-trick is even given a double-twist, so that *both* participants turn out to be substitutes. Although the theme of gambling sustains some of the now-expected topical interest, here the note of social criticism is muted, and there is even some sympathy for the values of courtly society – no doubt due to the intention to present the play before the king, who was said to have suggested its plot. Bentley found it surprising that 'there are no records of performance of *The Gamester* after the one at court', but perhaps the pragmatic shift in the play's moral focus is explanation enough.

Courtiers are once more put firmly in their places in *The Example* (1634), in which the detestable Lord Fitzavarice fails to purchase the favours of Lady Peregrine, and is scathingly but quite genuinely puzzled by her refusal to share his belief that sex is a negotiable commodity. Unfortunately, Fitzavarice's final repentance is even more than usually incredible after the perverse conviction of his sexual monetarism. Aretina in *The Lady of Pleasure* (1635) also undergoes a last-act conversion – to the honest, country values of her husband. But in the process of trying to curb her heedless emulation of courtly vices, the good Sir Thomas Barnwell discovers in Celestina a woman able to live in town and enjoy what it offers without sacrifice of honour or gentility. Butler reads into the play a clear preference for the cultivated code of behaviour represented by Celestina and 'the town' as opposed to the hedonistic tyranny of 'the court' to which Aretina aspires: but even if one cannot believe that either identification is quite so neat and convenient, it's certainly true that in *all* his London plays Shirley is concerned with *investigating* rather than *assuming* a code of morality, and in showing how that code changes according to social class and ambition. Less surprisingly, the sex of his characters also affects their attitudes, and although Shirley's gallery of independently-minded women tend to lapse conventionally in the last act into the arms of those they have previously and properly despised, at least for above four acts they view their menfolk with a scepticism that is both justified and refreshing. And that, too, is an unexpected reflection of the mood of the times.

Springtime in the Park

Hyde Park, one of the largest of London's open spaces, had its northern boundary fixed as early as Roman times, when the ancient way to Salisbury and Dorchester first traced the course which is still roughly followed by the Bayswater and Uxbridge Roads out of Oxford Street. After the Norman Conquest, the manor of Hyde was one of three comprising the estate of Eia, all of which were cultivated by the monks of Westminster Abbey until their dispossession by Henry VIII in 1536 – by which means the king secured for hunting an uninterrupted tract of land from his own palace of Westminster to Hampstead Heath. It was partly in order to rear and preserve the king's game that the park was now fenced in, occupying roughly its present area (including what were later to become Kensington Gardens). The works which created the Serpentine did not begin until 1730, though the original parkland was dotted with numerous ponds which were long a source of drinking water for the metropolis, and was also bisected by the Westbourne River – the bridge which spanned it on the south side of the park giving its name to the district of Knightsbridge. The sketch map, reproduced from a Civil War tract of 1642, shows Hyde and (to the north) Marylebone (later Regent's) Park, both far distant from the then built-up areas.

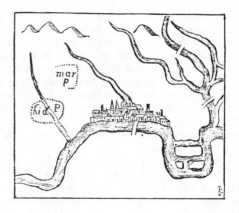

Before the Civil Wars, there were normally two keepers of the park, for one of whom the title was a sinecure. This sinecure passed in 1612 to Sir Henry Rich, who in 1624 became the Earl of Holland to whom Shirley so fulsomely dedicated his play – and who, being 'of a comely person', had been a great favourite of the sexually versatile James. Later suspected of too close an intimacy with Charles I's widely-hated wife Henrietta Maria, he turned his coat several times during the Civil Wars, and finally was executed by the parliamentarians in 1649.

It was during Holland's keepership that Hyde Park was first opened to the public, probably around the time that Shirley's play was first conceived. But the mention in his dedication of its being performed 'upon first opening of the Park' may refer only to the commencement of a new season, since the Park remained closed for the winter months. Shirley's editor Theodore Miles thus cites examples of 'Hyde Park time' as a topical synonym for the coming of warmer weather – while as soon as the third act of our play takes us to the Park, Lord Bonvile greets Julietta with a 'welcome to the spring'. Various other references, including the first appearance of the nightingale, stress the seasonal setting of *Hyde Park*.

The park quickly became a centre for sports, notably foot and horseracing, of which both James I and his son were resolute champions – Charles endorsing in 1634 his father's proclamation of the people's right to 'lawful recreation' on a Sunday, their only day of relative freedom from toil, despite the protests of the puritans. Occasional meetings for 'gentlemen's races' on horseback had been held in the reign of Elizabeth, but it was James I who truly popularised the 'sport of kings' – and made Newmarket, where many of his Scottish followers had settled, its national focus. His son was also anxious to promote the 'noble science' of riding, and extended Richmond Park for that purpose; but the averagely lazy Londoner found Hyde Park a more accessible venue, and one where the pleasures of gambling on the prowess of others quickly outweighed the attractions of taking one's own exercise.

Athletic sports in England were even older than the village greens on which they were usually held, but it was only in the seventeenth century that the nobility began to take an interest, and so to make foot-racing a fashionable spectator sport – wagers often being laid, as in our play, on the athletic abilities of the 'running footmen' now being hired by the sporting fancy. The not always reliable anecdotist John Evelyn relates how after watching one such race in Hyde Park Charles I publicly insulted the MP for Berkshire, Henry Martin, on account of his excessive wenching – for which Martin had a historic revenge when he set his name on Charles's death warrant in 1649. By that time, Hyde Park had long been closed to the public by the Civil Wars, and was intermittently the scene of military activity. 'Privatised' for a while during the Commonwealth, it was restored to Londoners along with their King in 1660, and, in the words of one ancient account, 'soon became again what it had been before the Civil Wars – the rendezvous of fashion'.

Marriage, Sex, and Social Class

The execution of Charles I in 1649 was at once a practical necessity and a political catastrophe for its perpetrators – not least in the Freudian sense that, for all the king's widely-acknowledged ineptitude, he was still 'the father of his people' and his beheading thus an unforgivable patricide. The monarch-as-patriarch was at the peak of a pyramidical social structure which relied for its stability on the acceptance of primogeniture, and descent through the male line. Paradoxically, therefore, the more the puritans insisted on the sanctification of 'holy matrimony', the more securely this patriarchal tradition was entrenched – and even the position of the king was enhanced in this one respect at least, since, as Roy Strong has put it, Charles and Henrietta Maria were 'the first English royal couple to be glorified as husband and wife in the domestic sense'. By comparison with the court of his father, the homosexual and concupiscent James I, not to mention that of his frankly libertine son, Charles's own court was a relatively respectable place, and even the queen cultivated nothing more ardent than neo-platonic love from her somewhat secluded circle of admirers.

But behaviour at court was only one of the influences on sexual behaviour in the Caroline period. While most marriages among the propertied classes were still arranged with economic and dynastic ends in view, prospective brides, though not actually able to choose their preferred husband, were at least able to veto a detested suitor. And it was the influence of puritanism which also began to call in question the 'double standard' which until quite recently had made it perfectly acceptable for a husband openly to keep a mistress, while permitting no indiscretion on the part of his wife. Fathers, meanwhile, were beginning to insist on some small financial independence for their daughters during their husband's lifetime, in addition to the jointure laid down in the marriage settlement in the event of his death. All too often, it was the wife's own death, frequently in childbirth, which ended one in three marriages within fifteen years; but the wife who survived to become a widow joined the only class of women able to dispose of themselves, if they so wished, at their own pleasure. Especially for a widower already supplied with that vital eldest son, a second marriage with a widow was often as attractive a catch financially as, by tradition, it was sexually. One side-effect of the idealization of matrimony, however, was that of replacing the respect traditional in a recently Catholic society for the virgin state with a contempt for spinsterhood and 'old maids'.

Even in the earlier years of the seventeenth century, marriages were predominantly local arrangements, but by the sixteen-thirties London was becoming established as the centre of marriage-brokerage as of other commercial transactions. Not only was there a superfluity of lawyers in the city to draw up settlements, but a pool of merchants willing to bargain wealth for entrance into the aristocracy – though with the ending of the sale of peerages by 1630 this particular means to upward mobility was just beginning to decline. Marriages were also being postponed to a slightly older age – the early twenties now more usual than the teens – but it was still not uncommon for a young man to be wed just a day or so before setting off on his foreign travels, with the intention of preventing an unsuitable match being contracted abroad. Such may even have been the situation of Bonavent in *Hyde Park* – the circumstance would at least explain the absence of children from his 'widow's' household – though in his case the travels were evidently intended for business, not pleasure.

In this as in other respects our play combines dramatic convenience with its accurate portrayal of social habits. Shirley seems to concern himself very little with his characters' background – and gives them no fathers or mothers trying to impose an arranged marriage, no guardians to propitiate, no humorous relations to indulge, and no 'ladies of a certain age' constantly dallying with mirror and makeup box. Everybody in *Hyde Park* down to servants, pages, and passing milkmaid is young and sexually alert – not least, perhaps, because the season is spring and traditionally associated (as are the origins of comedy itself) with the celebration of fertility and growth. Yet, as Kathleen McLuskie has observed, within Shirley's 'detailed portrayal of the leisured urban life . . . stripped of all trace of romance or melodrama', for these 'financially independent and assured young people,' love is 'merely another diversion'. If Lord Bonvile is a 'sprig of the nobility', for whom it is 'no shame . . . to love a wench', Lacy, though 'a man of pretty fortune', is gentleman enough to have proved an honest suitor to Mistress Bonavent. And she, from the social confidence of her bearing, must be presumed the superior of her missing husband, whose ungainly behaviour at the wedding feast only affirms his merchant origins. In the dramatic shorthand which Shirley employs (in peopling his play as in structuring it), relations of class and sex may often be subtextual – but they are untrue only in the independence of choice which Shirley (like Shakespeare before him) permits his female characters.

The Careful Structure of Inconsequence

Hyde Park is a deceptive play: of the three love chases it seems about to follow through, only one is successful – while if any modern audience settles into the comfortable expectation of meeting Restoration gulls and gallants before their time, it finds that none of the characters will quite slot into a ready-made typology. Fairfield and Carol, it's true, seem to belong to that recognisable tradition of bickering lovers which stretches from Shakespeare's Beatrice and Benedick to Congreve's Mirabell and Millamant and beyond. But when this couple hammer out their 'contract', it is a contract not to marry but to separate – and it is made as early as the second act, by which time Lacy and Mistress Bonavent also appear to have celebrated their marriage at least three acts too soon.

Again: if Trier and Julietta remind us retrospectively of Sheridan's Faulkland and Julia, this only serves to sharpen the jolt when the lady spurns her lover in the last act, in favour of the reformed Lord Bonvile – a turnabout which Martin Butler takes to be part of Shirley's optimistic social allegory. Julietta, he claims, is meant to embody the integrity of 'the town', and her eventual conversion of Bonvile thus represents the persuasion of 'the court' to accept the responsibilities which are the corollary of its power. Butler further suggests that the 'main antithesis' of the play is 'between nature and chance' – Carol's suitors, typically, treating her courtship as if it were a race in which one will defeat the others. Such interpretive niceties are almost impossible to predicate in terms of live theatre, but their relevance to an understanding of the apparently careless structure of the play is well worth following through.

More theatrically significant is Butler's suggestion that Hyde Park itself represents for Shirley 'a green world in urban London', and so is 'both country and town, nature and art'. This 'alternative nature' expresses the dual, town-and-country character 'of the gentry who frequent it and who are "cultivating" themselves' in the very pursuit of the social round. Despite the clear, eponymous importance of the park, it is, of course, the physical location only of the play's two middle acts: and in this, perhaps, Shirley is ironically tracing the familiar passage of much Shakespearian comedy, from court to country – and, inevitably, back again, the characters reconciled and refreshed by their experiences. But again Shirley breaks the mould, for Hyde Park is no pastoral Arden or mythic Athenian wood: it is merely a well-loved resort of fashionable Londoners, who seek only the 'refreshment' offered by Grave Maurice's Head in nearby Knightsbridge. And here most of the characters, obstinately or reluctantly, refuse to be 'reconciled' either.

This controlled microcosm of the countryside is, precisely, a place in which to *play games*, whether of amorous or athletic skill. We may lament that *Hyde Park* is no West End version of *Bartholomew Fair* – in which milkmaid, jockey, and Irish footman might have been expected to play a more instrumental part – yet within the limited social range on which he focuses, Shirley is just as intent as Jonson on observing the way in which people at play behave, and how the passing of their leisure time reflects their role in society. It was, of course, the mark of a gentleman that he was *always* at leisure – but the proper use and very justification of that leisure was the service of the state and the community. Butler's claim that Bonvile's dishonourable intentions towards Julietta put him in breach of the decorum which should govern his conduct as an aristocrat and a courtier is thus true enough – just as Trier breaches *his* decorum, as a reasonable gentleman about town, in misrepresenting his beloved as a 'lady of pleasure'.

For 'pleasure' is *not* synonymous with leisure, though Bonvile is in danger of confusing the two – just as the frequent, idiomatic use of the term 'servant' to signify not a household worker but an aspiring lover reflects ironically on the assumption held by most of the characters that nobody of importance need work for a living. But there is, of course, one person who does – the shadowy, disguised, but ultimately triumphant figure of the returned merchant, Bonavent. Shirley relaxes one kind of dramatic tension very early in the play by revealing Bonavent's existence, but in doing so he heightens tensions of quite another kind. Thus, we *know* that the 'marriage' of Lacy and Mistress Bonavent will prove to have been as much a 'game' as any of the antics in Hyde Park (and we are even reassured that the couple have not anticipated their marriage vows). Meanwhile, Bonavent, who could reassert his rights at any moment, is subjected to the social humiliation of being forced to join in the dancing – a social grace in which he is clearly unpractised. But while he bides his time, he knows that in this 'game' he holds all the trump cards. Even in the secret letter to his wife (which succinctly parodies every case-history of a traveller restored), he finds time to note that it was a 'worthy merchant' who 'redeemed and furnished' him home – just as Bonavent and his class were economically to 'redeem and furnish' their supposed betters with ever-increasing necessity as the years passed by.

The beginning of Shirley's play plunges us into the middle of one intrigue, catches the start of another, and celebrates the apparent climax to a third. And although it closes in anticipation of the reconciliatory feast traditional to comedy, it leaves almost all its characters – with the notable exception of the merchant and his wife – in a state of uncertainty. The parallels between dramatic and social states are uncannily exact, and the loose-ended quality of the play very much to the point. From Shirley's standpoint, the real 'climax' – the cataclysm of civil war – though only a decade away, could not be anticipated: yet buried none too deep in the deceptively simple, seemingly inconsequent structure of his play – with an art, like Jonson's in *Bartholomew Fair*, which conceals art – are many of the social tensions and uncertainties which brought that cataclysm about. Of course, this is a comedy, and so, although the uncertainties remain, the tensions are conventionally reconciled: the 'court' learns to reform its manners, and the 'town' to accept that 'country' values are best. But the 'city' snatches Lacy's newly-acquired property, sexual and substantial, from under his very nose. No wonder Bonavent is graceful enough to forgive the insult he has suffered, and invite everybody back to *his* house for supper with a mixture of generosity and enlightened self-interest. To Bonavent belongs the future.

For Further Reading

There has been no complete edition of Shirley's works since that edited in six volumes by W. Gifford and A. Dyce (London: John Murray, 1833), though this has now become more accessible in a facsimile reprint (New York: Russell, 1966). The one single-volume selection is a mere century old: edited by Edmund Gosse in the original Mermaid Series (London: Vizetelly, 1888), it does include *Hyde Park*, and does live up to its claim to be unexpurgated. *The Wedding* and *The Lady of Pleasure* are included in the anthology of *Six Caroline Plays*, edited by A. S. Knowland (London: Oxford University Press, 1962); while *The Triumph of Peace* and *Cupid and Death* are in *A Book of Masques*, edited by T. J. B. Spencer and Stanley Wells (Cambridge University Press, 1967). There are modern critical editions of *The Traitor* in the Regents Renaissance Drama Series (London: Arnold, 1965); and of *The Bird in a Cage, The Humorous Courtier, The Lady of Pleasure, Love's Cruelty, The Maid's Revenge, The Politician, St. Patrick for Ireland, The Wedding*, and *The Young Admiral* in the Renaissance Drama Series (New York: Garland, 1979 and 1980)

Critical attention to Shirley has been scant, although one recent full-length study, Ben Lucow's *James Shirley* in Twayne's English Authors Series (Boston: Twayne, 1981), provides a useful, more or less chronological introduction. The only biography remains A. H. Nason's *James Shirley, Dramatist* (New York: Nason, 1915; reprinted, New York: Blom, 1967), while the remaining full-length studies are out of date and of somewhat limited interest: they are R. S. Forsythe's *The Relations of Shirley's Plays to the Elizabethan Drama* (Columbia University Press, 1914; reprinted, New York: Blom, 1965); Hanson T. Parlin's *A Study in Shirley's Comedies of London Life* (Austin: University of Texas, 1914); and Stephen J. Radtke's *James Shirley: His Catholic Philosophy of Life* (Washington, DC: Catholic University of America, 1929).

Of the smattering of periodical literature, however, no less than three articles take *Hyde Park* as their main subject – Richard Levin's 'The Triple Plot of *Hyde Park*', in *Modern Language Review*, LXII (1967); Albert Wertheim's 'Games and Courtship in Shirley's *Hyde Park*', in *Anglia*, XC (1972); and Frieder Stadtfeld's 'Fortune, Providence, and Manners in James Shirley's *Hyde Park*', in *Anglia*, XCIII (1975). Theodore Miles's 'Place Realism in a Group of Caroline Plays', in *Review of English Studies*, XVIII (1942), and Nathan Cogan's 'James Shirley's *The Example*: Some Reconsiderations', in *Studies in English Literature*, XVII (1977), also touch on *Hyde Park;* while Juliet McGrath's 'James Shirley's Use of Language', in *Studies in English Literature*, VI (1966), and Marvin Morillo's 'Shirley's Preferment and the Court of Charles I', in *Studies in English Literature*, I (1961), are of more general, self-descriptive interest.

As will be clear from the many references to it in my commentary, one book to which all students of this writer and his times must be particularly indebted is Martin Butler's *Theatre and Crisis, 1632-1642* (Cambridge University Press, 1984) – in the light of which the previous major study, Alfred Harbage's still valuable *Cavalier Drama* (London: Oxford University Press, 1938) must now be read. Butler devotes an appendix to the polite but firm demolition of Ann Jennalie Cook's *The Privileged Play-goers of Shakespeare's London, 1576-1642* (Princeton University Press, 1981), which was itself intended to rebut Harbage's *Shakespeare's Audience* (New York: Columbia University Press, 1941). Clifford Leech's 'The Caroline Audience', in *Modern Language Review*, XXXVI (1942) and Michael Neill's 'Wit's Most Accomplished Senate: the Audience of the Caroline Private Theatres', in *Studies in English Literature*, XVIII (1978) remain worth reading alongside Butler, whose insights are also valuably complemented by Margot Heinemann in her *Puritanism and Theatre* (Cambridge University Press, 1980). Finally, the broader social and political context of the immediate pre-revolutionary period is dealt with in Lawrence Stone's classic study, *The Crisis of the Aristocracy, 1558-1641* (Oxford: Clarendon Press, 1965; abridged edition, 1967), which is far wider in scope than its title may suggest; and in the more controversial work of Christopher Hill, notably his *Intellectual Origins of the English Revolution* (Oxford: Clarendon Press, 1965).

James Shirley

HYDE PARK
by James Shirley

To the Right Honourable
Henry Earl of Holland,
Knight of the most noble Order of the Garter, one of his Majesty's most Honourable Privy Council, Chancellor of the University of Cambridge, &c.

My Lord,

The comedy, in the title, is a part of your lordship's command, which heretofore graced and made happy by your smile, when it was presented, after a long silence, upon first opening of the Park, is come abroad to kiss your lordship's hand. The applause it once received in the action, is not considerable with that honour your lordship may give it in your acceptance; that was too large, and might with some narrow and stoical judgment render it suspected: but this, depending upon your censure (to me above many theatres) is able to impart a merit to the poem, and prescribe opinion. If your lordship retired from business into a calm, and at truce with those high affairs wherein your counsel and spirit is fortunately active, vouchsafe to peruse these unworthy papers, you not only give a life to the otherwise languishing numbers, but quicken and exalt the genius of the author, whose heart pointeth at no greater ambition, than to be known,

My Lord,

to your name and honour,

the most humbly devoted,

James Shirley

Dramatis Personae

LORD BONVILE
FAIRFIELD ⎫
RIDER ⎬ amorous servants to MISTRESS CAROL
VENTURE ⎭
LACY, suitor to MISTRESS BONAVENT
TRIER suitor to JULIETTA
BONAVENT, a merchant, supposed to have been lost at sea
JARVIS, servant to MISTRESS BONAVENT
PAGE TO BONVILE
GENTLEMEN
JOCKEY
OFFICERS
RUNNERS
BAGPIPERS
PARK-KEEPERS, SERVANTS, &c
MISTRESS CAROL
MISTRESS BONAVENT, supposed to be a widow
JULIETTA, sister to FAIRFIELD
WAITING WOMAN
MILKMAID, &c

The Scene.
LONDON and HYDE PARK.

Street.
ter Trier and Lacy.

IER.
  And how, and how?

CY.
  The cause depends –

IER.
  No Mistress?

CY.
  Yes, but no wife.

IER.
  For now she is a widow.

CY.
  But I resolve –

IER.
  What does she say to thee?

CY.
  She says – I know not what she says – but I
  Must take another course; and yet she is –

IER.
  A creature of much sweetness, if all tongues
  Be just in her report; and yet 'tis strange,
  Having seven years expected, and so much
  Remonstrance of her husband's loss at sea,
  She should continue thus.

CY.
  What if she should
  Renew the bond of her devotion
  For seven years more?

IER.
  You will have time enough
  To pay in your affection.

CY.
  I would make
  A voyage to Cassandra's temple first,
  And marry a deformed maid; yet I must
  Confess, she gives me a fair respect.

TRIER.
  Has she
  A hope her husband may be living yet?

LACY.
  I cannot tell; she may have a conceit
  Some dolphin has preserved him in the storm,
  Or that he may be tenant to some whale,
  Within whose belly he may practise lent,
  And feed on fish till he be vomited
  Upon some coast: or, having 'scaped the seas,
  And bills of exchange failing, he might purpose
  To foot it o'er the Alps in his return,
  And by mischance is fallen among the mice
  With whom, perhaps, he battens upon sleep,
  Beneath the snow.

TRIER.
  This were a vagary.

LACEY.
  I know not what to think; or, is she not
  The worse for the coy lady that lives with her?

TRIER.
  Her kinswoman?

LACEY.
  Such a malicious piece,
  (I mean to love,) 'tis pity any place
  But a cold nunnery should be troubled with her.
  If all maids were but her disciples, we
  Should have no generation, and the world,
  For want of children, in few years undone by't:
  Here's one can tell you more. Is not that Jarvis,
  The widow's servant?

Enter Venture and Jarvis meeting.

VENTURE.   Whither in such haste, man?

JARVIS.
  I am commanded, sir, to fetch a gentleman.

VENTURE.
  To thy mistress? to give her a heat this morning?

JARVIS.
  I have spied him. – With your pardon –

  Goes to Lacy.

TRIER.
  Good morrow, Master Venture.

VENTURE

Frank Trier?

TRIER.

You
Look high and jocund, Venus has been propitious;
I dreamt last night thou wert a bridegroom.

VENTURE.

Such a thing may be; the wind blows now
From a more happy coast.

LACEY.

I must leave you; I am sent for.

TRIER.

To thy mistress?

LACEY.

Without more ceremony, gentlemen, my service.
Farewell.

Exit.

VENTURE.

I'll tell thee, I have a mistress.

TRIER.

I believe it.

VENTURE.

And yet I have her not.

TRIER.

But you have hope.

VENTURE.

Or rather certainty.

TRIER.

Why, I hear she is
A very tyrant over men.

VENTURE.

Worse, worse
The needle of a dial never had
So many waverings; but she is touched,
And she points only this way now, true north;
I am her pole.

TRIER.

And she your *Ursa minor*.

VENTURE.

I laugh to think how other of her rivals
Will look, when I enjoy her.

TRIER.

You are not yet contracted?

VENTURE.

No, she changed
Some amorous tokens; do you see this diamond?
A toy she gave me.

TRIER.

'Cause she saw you a spark.

VENTURE.

Her flame of love is here; and in exchange
She took a chain of pearl.

TRIER.

You'll see it hanged.

VENTURE.

These to the wise are arguments of love,
And mutual promises.

Enter Lord Bonvile and Page.

TRIER.

Your lordship's welcome to town:
I am blest to see your honour in good health.

LORD BONVILE.

Prithee visit my lodgings.

TRIER.

I shall presume to tender my humble service.

Exeunt Lord Bonvile and P

VENTURE.

What's he?

TRIER.

A sprig of the nobility,
That has a spirit equal to his fortunes;
A gentleman that loves clean napery.

VENTURE.

I guess your meaning.

TRIER.

A lady of pleasure; 'tis no shame for men
Of his high birth to love a wench; his honour
May privilege more sins: next to a woman,
He loves a running horse. –
Setting aside these recreations,
He has a noble nature, valient, bountiful.

NTURE.
I was of his humour till I fell in love,
I mean for wenching; you may guess a little,
By my legs; but I will now be very honest,
And when I am married –

IER.
Then you are confident
To carry away your mistress from them all?

NTURE.
From Jove himself, though he should practise all
His shapes to court her; 'tis impossible
She should have put any trick upon me, I
Have won her very soul.

IER.
Her body must
Needs be your own then.

NTURE.
I have a brace of rivals,
Would they were here, that I might jeer them!
And see how opportunely one is come!

Enter Rider.

I'll make you a little sport.

IER.
I have been melancholy,
You will express a favour in't.

DER.
Master Venture! the first man in my wish;
What gentleman is that?

NTURE.
A friend of mine.

DER.
I am his servant; look you, we are friends,
And't shall appear, however things succeed,
That I have loved you; and you cannot take
My counsel in ill part.

NTURE.
What is the business?

DER.
For my part, I have
Used no enchantment, philter, no devices
That are unlawful, to direct the stream
Of her affection; it flows naturally.

VENTURE.
How's this ? – (*Aside to Trier:*) Prithee observe.

TRIER.
I do, and shall laugh presently.

RIDER.
For your anger,
I wear a sword, though I have no desire
It should be guilty of defacing any
Part of your body; yet upon a just
And noble provocation, wherein
My mistress' love and honour is engaged,
I dare draw blood.

TRIER.
Ha, ha, ha!

VENTURE.
A 'mistress' love and honour!' this is pretty.

RIDER.
I know you cannot
But understand me; yet, I say I love you,
And with a generous breast, and in the confidence
You will take it kindly, I return to that
I promised you, good counsel; come, leave off
The prosecution.

VENTURE.
Of what, I prithee?

RIDER.
There will be less affront than to expect
Till the last minute, and behold the victory
Another's; you may guess why I declare this.
I am studious to preserve an honest friendship;
For though it be my glory, to be adorned
With trophies of her vanquished love –

VENTURE.
Whose love?

TRIER (*aside to Venture*).
This sounds as if he jeered you.

VENTURE (*drawing his sword*).
Mushroom!

TRIER.
What do you mean, gentlemen? friends and fall out
About good counsel!

VENTURE.
> I'll put up again,
> Now I think better on't.

TRIER.
> 'Tis done discreetly.
> Cover the nakedness of your tool, I pray.

VENTURE.
> Why, look you, sir; if you bestow this counsel
> Out of your love, I thank you; yet there is
> No great necessity, why you should be at
> The cost of so much breath; things well considered:
> A lady's love is mortal, I know that,
> And if a thousand men should love a woman,
> The dice must carry her; but one of all
> Can wear the garland.

TRIER.
> Now you come to him.

VENTURE.
> For my own part, I loved the lady well,
> But you must pardon me, if I demonstrate
> There's no such thing as you pretend, and therefor
> In quittance of your loving, honest counsel,
> I would not have you build an airy castle;
> Her stars have pointed her another way,
> This instrument will take her height.

Venture shows the diamond ring.

RIDER.
> Ha!

VENTURE.
> And you may guess what cause you have to triumph;
> I would not tell you this, but that I love you
> And hope you will not run yourself into
> The cure of Bedlam. He that wears this favour,
> Hath sense to apprehend.

RIDER.
> That diamond?

VENTURE.
> Observe it perfectly, there are no trophies
> Of vanquished love, I take it, coming toward you;
> 'It will be less affront, than to expect
> Till the last minute, and behold the victory
> Another's.'

RIDER.
> That ring I gave her.

TRIER.
> Ha, ha, ha!

VENTURE.
> This was his gift to her; ha, ha, ha!
> Have patience, spleen; ha, ha!

TRIER.
> The scene is changed!

RIDER.
> She will not use me thus; she did receive it
> With all the circumstance of love.

VENTURE.
> I pity him; my eyes run o'er. Dost hear? –
> I cannot choose but laugh, and yet I pity thee.
> She has a jeering wit, and I shall love her
> More heartily for this. What dost thou think?
> Poor gentleman, how he has fooled himself!

RIDER.
> I'll to her again.

VENTURE.
> Nay, be not passionate!
> I' faith, thou wert too confident, I knew
> It could not hold; dost think I'd say so much else?
> I can tell thee more; but lose her memory.

RIDER.
> Were it more rich.

He shows a chain of pearl.

> Than that which Cleopatra gave to Antony,
> With scorn I would return it.

TRIER.
> She give you this chain?

RIDER.
> She shall be hanged in chains ere I will keep it.

VENTURE.
> Stay, stay; let my eye
> Examine that – this chain? –

RIDER.
> Who would trust woman after this?

VENTURE.
> The very same

She took of me, when I received this diamond!

[RI]DER.
    Ha, ha! you do but jest; she will not fool
    You o' this fashion; look a little better,
    One may be like another.

[VE]NTURE.
    'Tis the same.

[RI]DER.
    Ha, ha! I would it were, that we might laugh
    At one another; by this hand I will
    Forgive her: prithee tell me – ha, ha, ha!

[R]IER.
    You will 'carry her
    From Jove himself, though he should practise all
    His shapes to court her.'

[RI]DER.
    By this pearl, – O rogue,
    How I do love her for't! – be not dejected;
    'A lady's love is mortal, one of all
    Must wear the garland; do not fool yourself
    Beyond the cure of Bedlam.'

[R]IER.
    She has fitted you
    With a pair of fools' coats, and as handsomely
    As any tailor, that had taken measure.

[VE]NTURE.
    Give me thy hand.

[R]IER.
    Nay, lay your heads together
    How to revenge it; and so, gentlemen,
    I take my leave.

                      Exit.

[VE]NTURE.
    She has abused us.

[RI]DER.
    Let us take his counsel;
    We can be but what we are.

[VE]NTURE.
    A pair of credulous fools.

[RI]DER.
    This other fellow, Fairfield, has prevailed.

VENTURE.
    Which if he have –

RIDER.
    What shall we do?

VENTURE.
    I think we were best let him alone.

RIDER.
    Do you hear? We'll to her again; (you will
    Be ruled by me); and tell her what we think of her.

VENTURE.
    She may come to herself, and be ashamed on't.

RIDER.
    If she would affect one of us, for my part
    I am indifferent.

VENTURE.
    So say I too, but to give us both the canvas! –
    Let's walk, and think how to behave ourselves.

                      Exeunt.

Scene Two

A Room in Bonavent's house.
Enter Mistress Bonavent and Mistress Carol.

MISTRESS CAROL.
    What do you mean to do with him?

MISTRESS BONAVENT.
    Thou art
    Too much a tyrant; the seven years are past,
    That did oblige me to expect my husband,
    Engaged to sea; and though within those limits
    Frequent intelligence hath reported him
    Lost, both to me, and his own life, I have
    Been careful of my vow; and were there hope
    Yet to embrace him, I would think another
    Seven years no penance: but I should thus
    Be held a cruel woman, in his certain
    Loss, to despise the love of all mankind.
    And therefore I resolve, upon so large
    A trial of his constancy, at last
    To give him the reward of his respects
    To me, and –

MISTRESS CAROL.
> Marry him.

MISTRESS BONAVENT.
> You have apprehended.

MISTRESS CAROL.
> No marvel if men rail upon you then,
> And doubt whether a widow may be saved.
> We maids are thought the worse on, for your easiness.
> How are poor women overseen! We must
> Cast away ourselves upon a whining lover,
> In charity: I hope my cousin's ghost
> Will meet you as you go to church, or if
> You 'scape it then, upon the wedding night –

MISTRESS BONAVENT.
> Fie! fie!

MISTRESS CAROL.
> When you are both abed, and candles out.

MISTRESS BONAVENT.
> Nay, put not out the candles.

MISTRESS CAROL.
> May they burn blue then, at his second kiss,
> And fright him from – well, I could say something;
> But take your course – He's come already.

Enter Lacy

> Put him off but another twelvemonth.

Mistress Bonavent walks aside with Lacy.

> So, so.
> Oh love, into what foolish labyrinths
> Dost thou lead us! I would all women were
> But of my mind, we would have a new world
> Quickly. I will go study poetry
> On purpose to write verses in the praise
> Of th' Amazonian ladies, in whom only
> Appears true valour (for the instruction
> Of all posterity) to beat their husbands.

LACY.
> How you endear your servant!

MISTRESS CAROL.
> I will not
> Be guilty of more stay.

Enter Fairfield.

FAIRFIELD.
> Sweet lady!

MISTRESS CAROL.
> You're come in time, sir, to redeem me.

FAIRFIELD.
> Why, lady?

MISTRESS CAROL.
> You will be as comfortable as strong waters;
> There's a gentleman –

FAIRFIELD.
> So uncivil to affront you?

MISTRESS CAROL.
> I had no patience to hear him longer;
> Take his offence, before you question him.

FAIRFIELD.
> And be most happy, if, by any service,
> You teach me to deserve your fair opinion.

MISTRESS CAROL.
> It is not civil to eavesdrop him, but
> I'm sure he talks on't now.

FAIRFIELD.
> Of what?

MISTRESS CAROL.
> Of love; is any thing more ridiculous?
> You know I never cherish that condition:
> In you 'tis the most harsh, unpleasing discord;
> But I hope you will be instructed better,
> Knowing how much my fancy goes against it
> Talk not of that, and welcome.

FAIRFIELD.
> You retain,
> I see, your unkind temper; will no thought
> Soften your heart? disdain agrees but ill
> With so much beauty; if you would persuade
> Me not to love you, strive to be less fair;
> Undo that face, and so become a rebel
> To heaven and nature.

MISTRESS CAROL.
> You do love my face then?

FAIRFIELD.
> As heavenly prologue to your mind; I do not
> Doat, like Pygmalion, on the colours.

MISTRESS CAROL.
No, you cannot; his was a painted mistress.
Or, if it be the mind you so pretend
To affect, you increase my wonder of your folly,
For I have told you that so often.

FAIRFIELD.
What?

MISTRESS CAROL.
My mind, so opposite to all your courtship,
That I had rather hear the tedious tales
Of Hollinshed, than any thing that trenches
On love. If you come fraught with any o'
Cupid's devices, keep them for his whirligigs;
Or load the next edition of his messenger,
Or post, with a mad packet, I shall but laugh
At them, and pity you.

FAIRFIELD.
That pity –

MISTRESS CAROL.
Do not mistake me, it shall be a very
Miserable pity, without love?
Were I a man, and had but half that handsomeness,
(For though I have not love, I hate detraction),
Ere I would put my invention to the sweat
Of compliment, to court my mistress' hand,
And call her smile, blessing beyond a sun-beam,
Entreat to wait upon her, give her rings
With wanton, or most lamentable poesies,
I would turn thrasher.

FAIRFIELD.
This is a new doctrine,
From women.

MISTRESS CAROL.
'Twill concern your peace, to have
Some faith in it.

FAIRFIELD.
You would not be neglected?

MISTRESS CAROL.
You neglect
Yourselves, the nobleness of your birth and nature,
By servile flattery of this jigging,
And that coy mistress; keep your privilege,
Your masculine property.

FAIRFIELD.
Is there so great
A happiness in nature?

MISTRESS CAROL.
There is one
(*Points to Lacy.*)
Just of your mind; can there be such happiness
In nature? Fie upon't, if it were possible,
That ever I should be so mad to love,
To which, I thank my stars, I am not inclined,
I should not hold such servants worth my garters,
Though they would put me in security
To hang themselves, and ease me of their visits.

FAIRFIELD.
You are a strange gentlewoman; why, look you, lady:
I am not so enchanted with your virtues,
But I do know myself, and at what distance
To look upon such mistresses; I can
Be scurvily conditioned; you are –

MISTRESS CAROL.
As thou dost hope for any good, rail now
But a little.

FAIRFIELD.
I could provoke you.

MISTRESS CAROL.
To laugh, but not to lie down. Why, prithee do.

FAIRFIELD.
Go, you are a foolish creature, and not worth
My services.

MISTRESS CAROL.
Aloud, that they may hear;
The more the merrier, I'll take't as kindly
As if thou hadst given me the Exchange. What, all this cloud
Without a shower?

FAIRFIELD.
You are most ingrateful.

MISTRESS CAROL.
Good!
Abominable peevish, and a wench
That would be beaten, beaten black and blue,
And then, perhaps, she may have colour for't.
Come, come, you cannot scold
With confidence, nor with grace; you should look big,
And swear you are no gamester; practise dice

And cards a little better, you will get
Many confusions and fine curses by't.

FAIRFIELD.
Is not she mad?

MISTRESS CAROL.
To show I have my reason,
I'll give you some good counsel, and be plain with you;
None that have eyes will follow the direction
Of a blind guide, and what do you think of Cupid?
Women are either fools, or very wise,
Take that from me; the foolish women are
Not worth your love, and if a woman know
How to be wise, she will not care for you.

FAIRFIELD.
Do you give all this counsel without a fee?
Come, be less wild. I know you cannot be
So hard of soul.

He offers to take her hand.

MISTRESS CAROL.
Prithee let my body alone!

FAIRFIELD.
Why are you thus peremptory? Had
Your mother been so cruel to mankind,
This heresy to love, with you had been
Unborn.

MISTRESS CAROL.
My mother was no maid.

FAIRFIELD.
How, lady?

MISTRESS CAROL.
She was married long ere I was born, I take it,
Which I shall never be, that rule's infallible;
I would not have you fooled in the expectation,
A favour all my suitors cannot boast of.
Go home, and say your prayers, I will not look
For thanks till seven year hence.

FAIRFIELD.
I know not what
To say; yes, I will home, and think a satire –
Was ever man jeered thus for his good will!

Exit.

MISTRESS BONAVENT.
The license will be soon, dispatched.

LACY.
Leave that
To my care, lady, and let him presume,
Whom you intend to bless with such a gift,
Seal on your lips the assurance o' his heart.

He kisses her.

I have more wings than Mercury: expect
Your servant in three minutes.

MISTRESS CAROL.
Take more time.
You'll overheat yourself, and catch a surfeit.

LACY.
My nimble lady, I have business; we
Will have a dialogue another time.

Ex

MISTRESS CAROL.
You do intend to marry him, then?

MISTRESS BONAVENT.
I have promised
To be his wife; and, for his more security,
This morning –

MISTRESS CAROL.
How! this morning?

MISTRESS BONAVENT.
What should one,
That has resolved, lose time? I do not love
Much ceremony; suits in love should not,
Like suits in law, be racked from term to term.

MISTRESS CAROL.
You will join issue presently, without your council,
You may be o'erthrown; take heed, I have known wives
That have been o'erthrown in their own case, and after
Nonsuited too, that's twice to be undone.
But take your course; some widows have been mortified.

MISTRESS BONAVENT.
And maids do now and then meet with their match.

MISTRESS CAROL.
What is in your condition makes you weary?
You are sick of plenty and command; you have
Too, too much liberty, too many servants;

Your jewels are your own, and you would see
How they will show upon your husband's wagtail.
You have a coach now, and a Christian livery
To wait on you to church, and are not catechised
When you come home; you have a waiting-woman,
A monkey, squirrel, and a brace of islands,
Which may be thought superfluous in your family,
When husbands come to rule. A pretty wardrobe,
A tailor of your own, a doctor too,
That knows your body, and can make you sick
I' the spring, or fall, or when you have a mind to't,
Without control; you have the benefit
Of talking loud and idle at your table,
May sing a wanton ditty, and not be chid
Dance, and go late to bed, say your own prayers,
Or go to Heaven by your chaplain.

STRESS BONAVENT.
    Very fine.

STRESS CAROL.
    And will you lose all this, for
'I, Cicely, take thee, John, to be my husband'?
Keep him still to be your servant;
Imitate me; a hundred suitors cannot
Be half the trouble of one husband. I
Dispose my frowns and favours like a princess;
Deject, advance, undo, create again;
It keeps the subjects in obedience,
And teaches 'em to look at me with distance.

Enter Venture and Rider.

STRESS BONAVENT.
    But you encourage some.

STRESS CAROL.
    'Tis when I have nothing else to do, for sport,
As, for example –

STRESS BONAVENT.
    But I am not now in tune to hear 'em; prithee
Let's withdraw.

                        Exeunt.

NTURE.
    Nay, nay, lady, we must follow you.

                 Exeunt Venture and Rider.

ACT TWO

Scene One
An outer Room in Bonavent's House.
Enter Bonavent in disguise, listening.

BONAVENT.
    Music and revels! they are very merry.

    Enter a Servant.

    By your favour, sir.

SERVANT.
    You are welcome.

BONAVENT.
    Pray, is this a dancing school?

SERVANT.
    No dancing school.

BONAVENT.
    And yet some voices sound like women.

SERVANT.
    Wilt please you
To taste a cup of wine? 'tis this day free
As at a coronation; you seem a gentleman.

BONAVENT.
    Prithee, who dwells here?

SERVANT.
    The house this morning was a widow's, sir,
But now her husband's; without circumstance,
She is married.

BONAVENT.
    Prithee, her name?

SERVANT.
    Her name was Mistress Bonavent.

BONAVENT.
    How long is't since her husband died?

SERVANT.
    'Tis two years since she had intelligence
He was cast away; at his departure, he
Engaged her to a seven years expectation,
Which full expired, this morning she became
A bride.

BONAVENT.
What's the gentleman she has married?

SERVANT.
A man of pretty fortune, that has been
Her servant many years.

BONAVENT.
How do you mean?
Wantonly? or does he serve for wages?

SERVANT.
Neither, I mean a suitor.

BONAVENT.
Cry mercy; may I be acquainted with his name?

SERVANT.
And his person too, if you have a mind to't;
Master Lacy; I'll bring you to him.

BONAVENT.
Master Lacy, may be 'tis he; would thou couldst help me to
A sight of this gentleman! I have business with
One of his name, and cannot meet with him.

SERVANT.
Please you walk in.

BONAVENT.
I would not be an intruder
In such a day; if I might only see him. –

SERVANT.
Follow me, and I'll do you that favour.

Exeunt.

Scene Two

Another Room in the same.
Enter Lacy, Mistress Bonavent, Rider, Mistress Carol and Venture,
dancing; followed at a distance by Bonavent.

VENTURE.
Who is that peeps?

LACY.
Peeps! – Who is that?

Bringing forward Bonavent.

– Faith, you shall dance.

BONAVENT.
Good sir, you must excuse me, I am a stranger.

LACY.
Your tongue does walk our language, and your feet
Shall do as we do: take away his cloak
And sword. – By this hand, you shall dance, Monsieur,
No *pardonnez moi.*

MISTRESS CAROL.
Well said, master bridegroom,
The gentleman may perhaps want exercise.

MISTRESS BONAVENT.
He will not take it well.

VENTURE.
The bridegroom's merry.

LACY.
Take me no takes;
Come, choose your firk, for dance you shall.

BONAVENT.
I cannot;
You'll not compel me?

LACY.
I have sworn.

BONAVENT.
'Tis an affront; as I am a gentleman,
I know not how to foot your chamber jigs.

LACY.
No remedy; here's a lady longs for one vagary. –
Fill a bowl of sack, and then to the Canaries.

BONAVENT.
You are circled with your friends, and do not well
To use this privilege to a gentleman's
Dishonour.

LACY.
You shall shake your heels.

BONAVENT.
I shall?
Ladies, it is this gentleman's desire
That I should make you mirth; I cannot dance,
I tell you that afore.

MISTRESS BONAVENT.
He seems to be a gentleman and a soldier.

STRESS CAROL.
  Good Mars, be not so sullen; you'll do more
  With Venus privately.

NAVENT.
  Because this gentleman is engaged, I'll try.

A dance.

  Will you excuse me yet?

CY.
  Play excuse me; yes, any thing you'll call for.

STRESS CAROL.
  This motion every morning will be wholesome
  And beneficial to your body, sir.

NAVENT.
  So, so.

STRESS CAROL.
  Your pretty lump requires it.

NAVENT.
  Where's my sword, sir? I have been your hobby-horse.

STRESS CAROL.
  You danced something like one.

NAVENT.
  Jeer on, my whimsy lady.

STRESS BONAVENT.
  Pray impute it
  No trespass studied to affront you, sir,
  But to the merry passion of a bridegroom.

CY.
  Prithee stay: we'll to Hyde Park together .

NAVENT.
  There you may meet with morris-dancers: for
  You, lady, I wish you more joy, so farewell.

                              Exit.

CY.
  Come, let's have t'other whirl, lustily, boys!

                         They dance off.

Scene Three

A Room in Fairfield's House.
Enter Fairfield, Julietta, and Waiting woman.

JULIETTA.
  You are resolved then?

FAIRFIELD.
  I have no other cure left,
  And if I do it not quickly, my affection
  May be too far spent, and all physic will
  Be cast away.

JULIETTA.
  You will show a manly fortitude.

FAIRFIELD.
  When saw you Master Trier?

JULIETTA.
  Not since yesterday.

FAIRFIELD.
  Are not his visits frequent?

JULIETTA.
  He does see me sometimes.

FAIRFIELD.
  Come, I know thou lov'st him, and he will
  Deserve it; he's a pretty gentleman.

JULIETTA.
  It was your character, that first commended
  Him to my thoughts.

FAIRFIELD.
  If he be slow to answer it,
  He loses me again; his mind, more than
  His fortune, gain'd me to his praise: but I
  Trifle my precious time.
  Farewell! all my good wishes stay with thee.

                         Exit Fairfield.

Enter Trier.

JULIETTA.
  And mine attend you! – Master Trier!

TRIER.
  I come to kiss your hand.

JULIETTA.
  And take your leave?

TRIER.

Only to kiss't again!

JULIETTA.

You begin to be a stranger; in two mornings
Not one visit, where you profess affection!

TRIER.

I should be surfeited with happiness
If I should dwell here.

JULIETTA.

Surfeits in the spring
Are dangerous, and yet I never heard,
A lover would absent him from his mistress
Through fear to be more happy; but I allow
That for a compliment, and dispute not with you
A reason of your actions. You are now welcome,
And though you should be guilty of neglect,
My love would overcome any suspicion.

TRIER.

You are all goodness –

Enter a Servant, and whispers Trier.

With me? prithee admit him

Exit Servant.

Enter Page.

PAGE.

Sir, my lord saw you enter, and desires
To speak with you.

TRIER.

His lordship shall command; where is he?

PAGE.

Below, sir.

TRIER.

Say, I instantly wait on him. –

Exit Page.

Shall I presume upon your favour, lady?

JULIETTA.

In what?

TRIER.

That I may entreat him hither? you will honour me
To bid him welcome; he is a gentleman
To whom I owe all services, and in
Himself is worthy of your entertainemtn.

JULIETTA.

If he be your's command me.

Enter Lord Bonvile and Page.

TRIER.

My lord, excuse –

LORD BONVILE.

Nay, I prevent your trouble. – Lady, I am
Your humble servant. – Pardon my intrusion.
I have no business, only I saw you enter.

TRIER.

Your lordship honours me.

LORD BONVILE.

What gentlewoman's this?

TRIER.

Why – (*Whispers to him.*)

LORD BONVILE.

A lady of pleasure! I like her eye, it has
A pretty twirl with't; will she bid one welcome?

TRIER.

Be confident, my lord. – Sweet lady, pray
Assure his lordship he is welcome.

JULIETTA.

I want words.

LORD BONVILE.

Oh, sweet lady, your lip in silence
Speaks the best language.

JULIETTA.

Your lordship's welcome to this humble roof.

LORD BONVILE (*aside*).

I am confirmed.

TRIER.

If you knew, lady, what
Perfection of honour dwells in him,
You would be studious, with all ceremony
To entertain him! besides, to me
His lordship's goodness hath so flowed, you cannot
Study, what will oblige me more than in
His welcome.

LORD BONVILE.

Come, you compliment.

JULIETTA.
> Though I want both ability and language,
> My wishes shall be zealous to express me
> Your humble servant.

LORD BONVILE.
> Come, that humble was
> But compliment in you, too.

JULIETTA.
> I would not
> Be guilty of dissembling with your lordship;
> I know words that have more proportion
> With my distance to your noble birth and fortune,
> Than humble servant.

LORD BONVILE.
> I do not love these distances.

TRIER (*aside*).
> You would have her be more humble. –
> This will try her,
> If she resist his siege, she is a brave one,
> I know he'll put her to't. He that doth love
> Wisely, will see the trial of his mistress,
> And what I want in impudence myself,
> Another may supply for my advantage;
> I'll frame excuse.

LORD BONVILE.
> Frank, thou art melancholy.

TRIER.
> My lord, I now reflected on a business
> Concerns me equal with my fortune, and
> It is the more unhappy that I must
> So rudely take my leave.

LORD BONVILE.
> What! not so soon?

TRIER.
> Your honour's pardon.

JULIETTA.
> Are you, sir, in earnest?

TRIER.
> Love will instruct you to interpret fairly;
> They are affairs that cannot be dispensed with. –
> I leave this noble gentleman.

JULIETTA.
> He's a stranger;

You will not use me well, and show no care
Of me, nor of my honour; I pray stay.

TRIER.
> Thou hast virtue to secure all; I am confident,
> Temptations will shake thy innocence
> No more than waves that climb a rock, which soon
> Betray their weakness, – and discover thee
> More clear and more impregnable.

JULIETTA.
> How is this?

TRIER.
> Farewell.
> I will not sin against your honour's clemency,
> To doubt your pardon.

LORD BONVILE.
> Well, an there by no remedy, I shall see you
> Anon in the Park; the match holds.

Exit Trier.

> I am not willing
> To leave you alone, lady.

JULIETTA.
> I have a servant.

LORD BONVILE.
> You have many; in their number pray write me,
> I shall be very dutiful.

JULIETTA.
> Oh, my lord.

LORD BONVILE.
> And when I have done a fault, I shall be instructed,
> But with a smile, to mend it.

JULIETTA.
> Done what fault?

LORD BONVILE.
> Faith, none at all, if you but think so.

JULIETTA.
> I think your lordship would not willingly
> Offend a woman.

LORD BONVILE.
> I would never hurt 'em,
> It has been my study still to please those women
> That fell within my conversation.

I am very tender-hearted to a lady,
I can deny them nothing.

JULIETTA.
    The whole sex
    Is bound to you.

LORD BONVILE.
    If they well considered things,
    And what a stickler I am in their cause,
    The common cause, but most especially
    How zealous I am in a virgin's honour,
    As all true knights should be, no woman could
    Deny me hospitality, and let down,
    When I desire access, the rude portcullice:
    I have a natural sympathy with fair ones,
    As they do, I do; there's no handsome woman
    Complains, that she has lost her maidenhead,
    But I wish mine had been lost with it.

JULIETTA.
    Your lordship's merry.

LORD BONVILE.
    'Tis because you look pleasant. –
    A very handsome lodging; is there any
    Accommodations that way.

JULIETTA.
    There's a garden,
    Will't please your lordship taste the air on't.

LORD BONVILE.
    I meant other conveniency; but if
    You please, I'll wait upon you thither.

                    Exeunt Lord Bonvile and Julietta.

PAGE.
    You and I had better stay, and in their absence
    Exercise one another.

WAITING WOMAN.
    How mean you, page?

PAGE.
    I'll teach you a way that we may follow 'em,
    And not remove from hence.

WAITING WOMAN.
    How, prithee?

PAGE.
    Shall I beg your lip?

WAITING WOMAN.
    I cannot spare it.

PAGE.
    I'll give you both mine.

WAITING WOMAN.
    What means the child?

PAGE.
    Because I have no upper lip, do you scorn me?
    I have kissed ladies before now, and have
    Been sent for to their chambers.

WAITING WOMAN.
    You sent for!

PAGE.
    Yes, and been trusted with their closets too!
    We are such pretty things, we can play at
    'All hid under a fardingale;' how long
    Have you been a waiting creature?

WAITING WOMAN.
    Not a month yet.

PAGE.
    Nay then, I cannot blame your ignorance;
    You have perhaps your maidenhead.

WAITING WOMAN.
    I hope so.

PAGE.
    Oh, lamentable! away with it, for shame.
    Chaffer it with the coachman, for the credit
    Of your profession; do not keep it long,
    'Tis fineable in court.

WAITING WOMAN.
    Good master page,
    How long have you been skilled in those affairs?

PAGE.
    E'er since I was in breeches; and you'll find
    Your honesty so troublesome.

WAITING WOMAN.
    How so?

PAGE.
    When you have trucked away your maidenhead,
    You have excuse lawful to put off gamesters,
    For you may swear, and give 'em satisfaction,
    You have not what they looked for; beside the benefit

Of being impudent as occasion serves,
A thing much in request with waiting creatures:
We pages can instruct you in that quality,
So you be tractable.

AITING WOMAN.
The boy is wild.

GE.
And you will lead me a chase, I'll follow you.

Exeunt.

ene Four

Room in Bonavent's House.
nter Mistress Carol, Rider, and Venture.

STRESS CAROL.
Why, did you ever think I could affect,
Of all men living, such a thing as you are?
What hope, or what encouragement did I give you?
Because I took your diamond, must you presently
Bound like a stoned horse?

DER.
She's a very colt.

STRESS CAROL.
'Cause you can put your hat off like a dancer,
And make a better leg than you were born to,
For, to say truth, your calf is well amended,
Must this so overtake me, that I must
Straight fall in love with you? one step to church.
Another into the streets? more to a bargain;
You are wide a bow, and something overshot.

NTURE.
Then this is all that I must trust to, you
Will never have me?

STRESS CAROL.
In my right mind, I think so.
Why, prithee tell me, what I should do with thee?

NTURE.
Can you find nothing to do with me?

STRESS CAROL.
To find my monkey spiders, were an office,
Perhaps, you would not execute?

VENTURE.
You are a gipsy,
And none of the twelve Sybils in a tavern,
Have such a tanned complexion; there be dogs
And horses in the world.

MISTRESS CAROL.
They'll keep you company.

VENTURE.
Tell me of spiders!
I'll wring your monkey's neck off.

MISTRESS CAROL.
And then puzzle
Your brain to make an elegy, which shall be sung
To the tune of 'The Devil and the Baker;' good!
You have a pretty ambling wit in summer;
Do you let it out, or keep't for your own riding?
Who holds your stirrup, while you jump
Into a jest, to the endangering
Of your ingenious quodlibets?

RIDER.
Come, thou hast said enough.

MISTRESS CAROL.
To him; you would have some?

RIDER.
Some testimony of your love, if it please you.

MISTRESS CAROL.
Indeed, I have heard you are a precious gentleman,
And in your younger days could play at trap well.

RIDER.
Fare you well, gentlewoman! by this light a devil;
I'll follow my old game of horse-racing.

VENTURE.
I could tear her ruff! I would thou wert
A whore, then I'd be revenged, and bring the 'prentices
To arraign thee on Shrove Tuesday; a pox upon you!

Enter Fairfield.

MISTRESS CAROL.
A third man, a third man! two fair gamesters;

RIDER.
For shame! let's go.

MISTRESS CAROL.
Will you stay, gentlemen? you have no more wit

Exeunt Venture and Rider.

To vent! keep your heads warm in any case,
There may be dregs in the bottom o' the brain pan,
Which may turn to somewhat in seven years; and set
You up again. – Now, sir.

FAIRFIELD.
Lady, I am come to you.

MISTRESS CAROL.
It does appear so.

FAIRFIELD.
To take my leave.

MISTRESS CAROL.
'Tis granted, sir; good bye.

FAIRFIELD.
But you must stay and hear a little more.
I promise not to trouble you with courtship,
I am as weary as you can be displeased with't,

MISTRESS CAROL.
On these conditions, I would have the patience
To hear the brazen head speak.

FAIRFIELD.
Whether, or how I purpose to dispose
Myself hereafter, as I know you have
No purpose to enquire, I have no great
Ambition to discourse; but how I have
Studied your fair opinion, I remit
To time, and come now only to request
That you would grant, in lieu of my true service,
One boon at parting.

MISTRESS CAROL.
Fort bon! proceed.

FAIRFIELD.
But you must swear to perform truly what
I shall desire; and that you may not think
I come with any cunning to deceive you,
You shall accept whate'er you would deny me;
And after all, I'll make request.

MISTRESS CAROL.
How's this?

FAIRFIELD.
But it concerns my life, or what can else
Be nearer to me, that you swear.

MISTRESS CAROL.
To what?

FAIRFIELD.
When you have made exceptions, and thought
What things in all the world you will exempt
From my petition, I'll be confident
To tell you my desire.

MISTRESS CAROL.
This is fair play.

FAIRFIELD.
I would not for an empire, by a trick
Oblige you to perform what should displease you.

MISTRESS CAROL.
'Tis a very strange request; are you in earnest?
Ere you begin, shall I except? 'tis odds
But I may include, what you have a mind to, then
Where's your petition?

FAIRFIELD.
I will run that hazard.

MISTRESS CAROL.
You will? why, look you; for a little mirth's sake,
And since you come so honestly, because
You shall not say, I am composed of marble,
I do consent.

FAIRFIELD.
Swear.

MISTRESS CAROL.
I am not come to that;
I'll first set bounds to your request, and when
I have left nothing for you worth my grant,
I'll take a zealous oath to grant you any thing.

FAIRFIELD.
You have me at your mercy.

MISTRESS CAROL.
First, you shall not
Desire that I should love you.

FAIRFIELD.
That's first; proceed.

MISTRESS CAROL.
No more but 'proceed'? Do you know what I say?

FAIRFIELD.
Your first exception forbids to ask

That you should love me.

MISTRESS CAROL.
And you are contented?

FAIRFIELD.
I must be so.

MISTRESS CAROL (*aside*).
What, in the name of wonder, will he ask me?
You shall not desire me to marry you.

FAIRFIELD.
That's the second.

MISTRESS CAROL.
You shall neither directly nor indirectly, wish me to lie with
you.
Have I not clipt the wings of your conceit?

FAIRFIELD.
That's the third.

MISTRESS CAROL.
'That's the third!' is there any thing a young man would
Desire of his mistress, when he must neither love, marry, nor
lie with her?

FAIRFIELD.
My suit is still untouched.

MISTRESS CAROL.
Suit! if you have another 'tis out of fashion,
You cannot beg my state, yet I would willingly
Give part of that, to be rid of thee.

FAIRFIELD.
Not one jewel.

MISTRESS CAROL.
You would not have me spoil my face, drink poison,
Or kill any body?

FAIRFIELD.
Goodness forbid, that I should wish you danger!

MISTRESS CAROL.
Then you would not have me ride through the city naked,
As once a princess of England did through Coventry?

FAIRFIELD.
All my desires are modest.

MISTRESS CAROL.
You shall not beg my parrot, nor entreat me
To fast, or wear a hairy smock.

FAIRFIELD.
None of these.

MISTRESS CAROL.
I will not be confined to make me ready
At ten, and pray till dinner; I will play
At gleek as often as I please, and see
Plays when I have a mind to't, and the races,
Though men should run Aldamites before me.

FAIRFIELD.
None of these trench on what I have to ask.

MISTRESS CAROL.
Why, then I swear – stay,
You shall not ask me before company
How old I am, a question most untoothsome.
I know not what to say more; I'll not be
Bound from Spring-garden, and the 'Sparagus.
I will not have my tongue tied up, when I've
A mind to jeer my suitors, among which
Your worship shall not doubt to be remembered,
For I must have my humour, I am sick else;
I will not be compelled to hear your sonnets,
A thing before I thought to advise you of;
Your words of hard concoction, your rude poetry,
Have much impaired my health, try sense another while
And calculate some prose according to
The elevation of our pole at London,
As says the learned almanack – but, come on,
And speak your mind, I have done; I know not what
More to except; if it be none of these,
And, as you say, feasible on my part,
I swear.

FAIRFIELD.
By what?

MISTRESS CAROL.
For once, a kiss, it may be a parting blow.
By that I will perform what you desire.

She kisses him.

FAIRFIELD.
In few words thus receive it: by that oath
I bind you never to desire my company
Hereafter; for no reason to affect me;
This, I am sure, was none of your exceptions.

MISTRESS CAROL.
What has the man said?

FAIRFIELD.
>'Tis clear, I am confident,
>To your understanding.

MISTRESS CAROL.
>You have made me swear
>That I must never love you, nor desire
>Your company.

FAIRFIELD.
>I know you will not violate
>What you have sworn, so all good thoughts possess you.

>>*Exit Fairfield.*

MISTRESS CAROL.
>Was all this circumstance for this? I never
>Found any inclination to trouble him
>With too much love; why should he bind me from it,
>And make me swear? an oath that, for the present,
>I had no affection to him, had been reasonable;
>But for the time to come, never to love,
>For any cause or reason, that may move me
>Hereafter, very strange! I know not what to think on't,
>Although I never meant, to think well of him,
>Yet to be limited, and be prescribed,
>I must not do it, – 'twas a poor trick in him;
>But I'll go practise something to forget it.

>>*Exit Mistress Carol.*

ACT THREE

Scene One

A part of Hyde Park.
Enter Lord Bonvile and Julietta.

LORD BONVILE.
>Lady, you are welcome to the spring; the Park
>Looks fresher to salute you: how the birds
>On every tree sing, with more cheerfulness
>At your access, as if they prophesied
>Nature would die, and resign her providence
>To you, fit only to succeed her!

JULIETTA.
>You express
>A master of all compliment; I have
>Nothing but plain humility, my lord,
>To answer you.

LORD BONVILE.
>But I'll speak our own English,
>Hang these affected strains, which we sometimes
>Practise, to please the curiosity
>Of talking ladies; by this lip thou'rt welcome, (*Kisses her.*)
>I'll swear a hundred oaths upon that book,
>An't please you.

Enter Trier, behind.

TRIER.
>They are at it.

JULIETTA.
>You shall not need, my lord, I'm not incredulous,
>I do believe your honour, and dare trust
>For more than this.

LORD BONVILE.
>I will not break my credit
>With any lady that dares trust me.

JULIETTA.
>She had a cruel heart, that would not venture
>Upon the engagement of your honour.

LORD BONVILE.
>What?
>What durst thou venture now, and be plain with me?

JIETTA.
There's nothing in the verge of my command,
That should not serve your lordship.

RD BONVILE.
Speak, speak truth,
And flatter not, on what security?

JIETTA.
On that which you propounded, sir, your honour:
It's above all other obligation,
And he that's truly noble, will not stain it.

RD BONVILE.
Upon my honour will you lend me then
But a night's lodging?

JIETTA.
How, sir?

RD BONVILE (*aside*).
She is angry;
I shall obtain, I know the trick on't; had
She yielded at the first, it had been fatal.

JIETTA.
It seems your lordship speaks to one you know not.

RD BONVILE.
But I desire to know you better, lady.

JIETTA.
Better I should desire, my lord.

RD BONVILE.
Better or worse, if you dare venture one,
I'll hazard t'other.

JIETTA.
'Tis your lordship's mirth.

RD BONVILE.
You're in the right, 'tis the best mirth of all.

JIETTA.
I'll not believe, my lord, you mean so wantonly
As you profess.

RD BONVILE.
Refuse me, if I do not.
Not mean? I hope you have more charity
Than to suspect, I'll not perform as much,
And more than I have said; I knew my fault,
I am too modest when I undertake,
But when I am to act, let me alone.

TRIER (*comes forward*).
You shall be alone no longer. –
My good lord.

LORD BONVILE.
Frank Trier.

TRIER.
Which side holds your honour

LORD BONVILE.
I am o' thy side, Frank.

TRIER.
I think so,
For all the Park's against me; but six to four
Is odds enough.

JULIETTA.
Is it so much against you?

TRIER.
Lady, I think 'tis two to one.

LORD BONVILE.
We were on even terms till you came hither. –
I find her yielding. – And when do they run?

TRIER.
They say presently.

LORD BONVILE.
Will you venture anything, lady?

TRIER.
Perhaps she reserves herself for the horse-race.

JULIETTA (*aside*).
There I may venture somewhat with his lordship.

LORD BONVILE.
That was a witty one.

TRIER.
You will be doing.

LORD BONVILE.
You are for the footmen.

TRIER.
I run with the company.

Enter Rider and Venture.

VENTURE.
I'll go your half.

RIDER.
No, thank you, Jack; would I had ten pieces more on't!

LORD BONVILE.
Which side?

RIDER.
On the Irishman.

LORD BONVILE.
Done; I'll maintain the English.
As many more with you;
I have to cherish our own countrymen.

VENTURE.
'Tis done, my lord.

TRIER.
I'll rook for once; my lord,
I'll hold you twenty more.

LORD BONVILE.
Done with you, too.

JULIETTA.
Your lordship is very confident.

LORD BONVILE.
I'll lay with you, too.

TRIER (*aside*).
Lie with her, he means.

LORD BONVILE.
Come; you shall venture something.
What gold against a kiss? but if you lose,
You shall pay it formally down upon my lip.

TRIER.
Though she should win, it would be held extortion
To take your money.

JULIETTA.
Rather want of modesty,
A greater sin, if you observe the circumstance.
I see his lordship has a disposition
To be merry, but proclaim not this free lay
To every one; some women in the world
Would hold you all day.

LORD BONVILE.
But not all night, sweet lady.

VENTURE.
Will you not see them, my lord?

LORD BONVILE.
Frank Trier, you'll wait upon this gentlewoman;
I must among the gamesters, I shall quickly
Return to kiss your hand.

Exit Bonv

TRIER.
How do you like this gallant?

JULIETTA.
He's one it becomes not me to censure.

TRIER.
Do you not find him coming? a wild gentleman;
You may in time convert him.

JULIETTA.
You made me acquainted with him to that purpose,
It was your confidence; I'll do what I can,
Because he is your noble friend, and one
In whom was hid so much perfection
Of honour, for at first 'twas most invisible,
But it begins to appear, and I do perceive
A glimmering, it may break out a flame,
I shall know all his thoughts at our next conference;
He has a secret to impart, he says,
Only to me.

TRIER.
And will you hear it?

JULIETTA.
Yes, sir;
If it be honourable, there is no harm in't,
If otherwise, you do not doubt my innocence.

TRIER.
But do not tempt a danger.

JULIETTA.
From his lordship?

TRIER.
I do not say from him.

JULIETTA.
From mine own frailty?

TRIER.
I dare not conclude that, but from the matter
Of his discourse, on which there may depend
A circumstance, that may not prove so happy.

JULIETTA.
Now I must tell you, sir, I see your heart
Is not so just as I deserve; you have
Engaged me to this conversation,
Provoked by jealous thoughts, and now your fear
Betrays your want of goodness, for he never
Was right at home, that dare suspect his mistress.
Can love degenerate in noble breasts?
Collect the arguments, that could invite you
To this unworthy trial, bring them to
My forehead, where you shall inscribe their names
For virgins to blush at me, if I do not
Fairly acquit myself.

TRIER.
Nay, be not passionate.

JULIETTA.
I am not, sir, so guilty to be angry;
But you shall give me leave, unless you will
Declare, you dare not trust me any further,
Not to break off so rudely with his lordship.
I will hear what he means to say to me,
And if my counsel may prevail with you,
You shall not interrupt us; have but patience,
I'll keep the story for you, and assure
My ends have no base mixture, nor my love
To you could bribe me to the least dishonour,
Much less a stranger; since I have gone so far
By your commission, I will proceed
A little further, at my peril, sir.

TRIER.
I know thou art proof against a thousand engines.
Pursue what ways you please.

They walk aside.
Enter Lacy, Mistress Bonavent, Mistress Carol, and Servant.

JULIETTA.
This morning married? –

TRIER.
That's your brother's mistress.

JULIETTA.
She that jeers
All within gun-shot?

TRIER.
In the way of suitors,
She is reported such a tyrant.

JULIETTA.
My brother.

Enter Fairfield.

FAIRFIELD.
Frank Trier.

JULIETTA.
Brother, do you know that gentlewoman?

FAIRFIELD.
'Tis she; then you and I must seem more familiar,
And you – (*To Lacy:*) – shall not be angry.

LACY.
What gentlewoman's that?

TRIER.
She does not know thee.

MISTRESS CAROL (*seeing Fairfield and Julietta*).
– Was this his reason? (*Aside.*) – Pray, if you love me, let's
Walk by that gentleman.

LACY.
Master Fairfield.

MISTRESS CAROL.
Is that well-trussed gentleman one of them that run?

MISTRESS BONAVENT.
Your sweetheart.

MISTRESS CAROL.
Ha, ha! I'd laugh at that.
If you allow a bushel of salt to acquaintance,
Pray vouchsafe two words to a bargain, while you live,
I scarce remember him. – (*Aside.*) Keep in, great heart.

Enter Bonavent.

LACY.
Oh sir, you are very well met here.

BONAVENT.
We are met indeed, sir; thank you for your music.

LACY.
It is not so much worth.

BONAVENT.
I made you merry, Master Bridegroom.

LACY.
I could not choose but laugh.

BONAVENT.
 Be there any races here?

LACY.
 Yes, sir, horse and foot.

BONAVENT.
 You'll give me leave to take my course, then.

MISTRESS CAROL.
 This is the captain that did dance.

BONAVENT.
 Not so nimbly as your wit; pray let me ask you a question,
 (Takes Mistress Carol aside.)
 I hear that gentlewoman's married.

MISTRESS CAROL.
 Married! without question, sir.

BONAVENT.
 Do you think he has been aforehand?

MISTRESS CAROL.
 How do you mean?

BONAVENT.
 In English, has he played the forward gamester,
 And turned up trump?

MISTRESS CAROL.
 Before the cards be shuffled? –
 I lay my life you mean a coat card.
 Deal again, you gave one too many
 In the last trick, yet I'll tell you what I think.

BONAVENT.
 What?

MISTRESS CAROL.
 I think she and you might have shown more wit.

BONAVENT.
 Why she and I?

MISTRESS CAROL.
 She to have kept herself a widow, and you
 Not to have asked me such a foolish question;
 But if she had been half so wise, as in
 My conscience she is honest, you have missed
 That excellent occasion, to show
 Your notable skill in dancing; but it pleased
 The learned Destinies to put things together,
 And so we separate.

 They come forward.

BONAVENT.
 Fare you well, mistress.

MISTRESS CAROL (*to Rider*).
 – Come hither; go to that gentleman, Master Fairfiel
 (*Whispers him.*)

MISTRESS BONAVENT.
 Prithee, sweetheart, who runs?

LACY.
 An Irish and an English footman.

MISTRESS BONAVENT.
 Will they run this way?

LACY.
 Just before you; I must have a bet.

Exit La

MISTRESS BONAVENT.
 Nay, nay; you shall not leave me.

MISTRESS CAROL.
 Do it discreetly;

Exit Ria

 (*Aside.*) I must speak to him,
 To ease my heart, I shall burst else,
 We'll expect 'em here. – Cousin, do they run naked?

MISTRESS BONAVENT.
 That were a most immodest sight.

MISTRESS CAROL.
 Here have been such fellows, cousin.

MISTRESS BONAVENT.
 It would fright the women.

MISTRESS CAROL.
 Some are of opinion it brings us hither.

 Noise within.

 Hark, what a confusion of tongues there is!
 Let you and I venture a pair of gloves
 Upon their feet; I'll take the Irish.

MISTRESS BONAVENT.
 'Tis done; but you shall pay if you lose.

MISTRESS CAROL.
 Here's my hand, you shall have the gloves, if you win.

 (*A cry within:*) A Teague! a Teague! Make way, for shame!

STRESS BONAVENT.
    I think they are started.

The two Runners cross the stage, followed by Lord Bonvile,
Venture, and others.

RD BONVILE.
    I hold any man forty pieces, yet.

NTURE.
    A hundred pounds to ten! a hundred pieces to ten! will no man
        take me?

NAVENT.
    I hold you, sir.

NTURE.
    Well, you shall see. –

(*Within:*) A Teague! a Teague! hey!

IER.
    Ha! well run Irish!

            Exeunt all but Mistress Carol and Mistress Bonavent.

STRESS BONAVENT.
    He may be in a bog anon.

STRESS CAROL.
    Can they tell what they do in this noise?
    Pray Heaven it do not break into the tombs
    At Westminster, and wake the dead.

Re-enter Fairfield and Julietta.

IRFIELD.
    She's yonder still, she thinks thee a new mistress.

LIETTA.
    I observe her.

Re-enter Trier.

IRFIELD.
    How go things, Frank?
    Prithee, observe that creature.

IER.
    She leers this way.

IRFIELD.
    I have done such a strange cure upon her!
    She has sent for me, and I entreat thee, Frank,
    To be a witness of my triumph; 'tis
    Now in my power to punish all her jeers;
    But I'll go to her: thou shalt keep at distance,

Only to hear how miraculously
I have brought things about.

TRIER.
    The cry returns.

                        Exeunt Fairfield and Trier.

(*Within:*) Make way there! a Teague! a Teague! a Teague!

The two Runners re-cross the stage, followed by Lord Bonvile,
Venture, Bonavent, etc.

VENTURE.
    Forty, fifty, a hundred pieces to ten!

BONAVENT.
    I hold you.

VENTURE.
    Well, you shall see, you shall see.

BONAVENT.
    This gentleman does nothing but talk; he makes good no bet.

VENTURE.
    Talk? You prate; I'll make good what I please, sir.

BONAVENT.
    Make the best you can of that.

They switch, and then draw.

MISTRESS BONAVENT.
    For Heaven's sake, let's remove.

MISTRESS CAROL.
    What! for a naked weapon?

                Exeunt Mistress Bonavent and Mistress Carol.

LORD BONVILE.
    Fight, gentlemen,
    You are fine fellows, 'tis a noble cause. –

                        Exeunt Venture and Bonavent.

Come, lady, I'll discharge your fears.
A cup of sack, and Anthony at the Rose.
Will reconcile their furies.

                        Exeunt Bonvile and Julietta.

Scene Two

Another part of the Park.
Enter Fairfield and Trier.

FAIRFIELD.
>I make a doubt whether I should go to her,
>Upon a single summons.

TRIER.
>By any means.

FAIRFIELD.
>What women are forbidden
>They're made to execute; she's here, be you
>In the reach of her voice, and see how I will humble her.

Enter Mistress Carol and Rider.

MISTRESS CAROL.
>But keep at some fit distance.

RIDER.
>You honour me, and shall
>Command me any service.

>>>>*Exit Rider.*

MISTRESS CAROL (*aside*).
>He has gone a strange way to work with me.

FAIRFIELD.
>Well advised; observe and laugh, without a noise.

Trier drops behind.

MISTRESS CAROL (*aside*).
>I am ashamed to think what I must say now.

FAIRFIELD.
>By your leave, lady! I take it you sent for me?

MISTRESS CAROL.
>You will not be so impudent? I send for you!
>By whom, or when?

FAIRFIELD.
>Your servant –

MISTRESS CAROL.
>Was a villain, if he mentioned
>I had any such desire; he told me, indeed,
>You courted him to entreat me, that I would
>Be pleased to give you another audience,
>And that you swore, I know not what, confound you,
>You would not trouble me above six words.

FAIRFIELD.
>You are prettily disposed.

MISTRESS CAROL.
>With much ado, you see, I have consented.
>What is it you would say?

FAIRFIELD.
>Nay, what is't you would say?

MISTRESS CAROL.
>Have you no prompter, to insinuate
>The first word of your studied oration? –
>He's out on's part. – Come, come, I will imagine it,
>Was it not something to this purpose – 'Lady,'
>Or 'Mistress,' or what you will, 'although
>I must confess, you may with justice laugh at
>My most ridiculous suit, and you will say
>I am a fool –'

FAIRFIELD.
>You may say any thing.

MISTRESS CAROL.
>'To come again, whom you have so tormented;
>For ne'er was simple camomile so trod on,
>Yet still I grow in love; but since there is
>No hope to thaw your heart, I now am desperate;
>Oh give me, lend me but the silken tie
>About your leg, which some do call a garter,
>To hang myself, and I am satisfied.'
>Am I not a witch?

FAIRFIELD.
>I think thou art past it.
>Which of the Furies art though made already?
>I shall depart the world, ne'er fear it, lady,
>Without a necklace. Did not you send for me?

TRIER.
>I shall laugh aloud sure.

MISTRESS CAROL.
>What madness has possessed you? have I not sworn,
>You know by what, never to think well of you,
>Of all men living, not to desire your company?
>And will you still intrude? Shall I be haunted
>For ever? no place give me privilege?
>Oh man, what art thou come to?

FAIRFIELD.
>Oh woman!
>How far thy tongue and heart do live asunder!

Come, I have found you out; off with this veil,
It hides not your complexion; I do tell thee,
I see thy heart, and every thought within it;
A little peevishness, to save your credit,
Had not been much amiss, but this over-
Over-doing the business, – it appears
Ridiculous, like my suit, as you inferred;
But I forgive thee, and forget thy tricks
And trillabubs, and will swear to love thee heartily;
Wenches must have their ways.

MISTRESS CAROL.

Pardon me, sir, if I have seemed too light;
It was not rudeness from my heart, but a
Disguise to save my honour, if I found
You still incredulous.

FAIRFIELD.

I love thee better
For thy vagaries.

MISTRESS CAROL.

In vain, I see, I should dissemble with you,
I must confess you have caught me; had you still
Pursued the common path, I had fled from you;
You found the constitution of women
In me, whose will, not reason, is their law;
Most apt do do, what most they are forbidden,
Impatient of curbs, in their desires.

FAIRFIELD.

Thou say'st right,

MISTRESS CAROL.

Oh love, I am thy captive; –
But I am forsworn, am I not, sir?

FAIRFIELD.

Ne'er think of that.

MISTRESS CAROL.

Ne'er think on't!

FAIRFIELD.

'Twas a vain oath, and well may be dispensed with.

MISTRESS CAROL.

Oh, sir, be more religious; I never
Did violate an oath in all my life;
Though I have been wild, I had a care of that.
An oath's a holy obligation,
And never dreaming of this chance, I took it
With true intention to perform your wishes.

FAIRFIELD.

'Twas but a kiss, I'll give it thee again.

MISTRESS CAROL.

But 'tis enrolled in that high court already.
I must confess, I could look on you now
With other eyes, for my rebellious heart
Is soft and capable of love's impression;
Which may prove dangerous, if I cherish it,
Having forsworn your love.

FAIRFIELD.

Now I am fitted!
I have made twigs to jerk myself. (*Aside.*) – Well thought on!
You shall absolve yourself; your oath does not
Oblige you to perform what you excepted,
And among them, if you remember, you
Said you must have your humour, you'd be sick else;
Now, if your humour be to break your oath,
Your obligation's void.

MISTRESS CAROL.

You have relieved me!
But do not triumph in your conquest, sir,
Be modest in your victory.

FAIRFIELD.

Will not you
Fly off again, now you're at large?

MISTRESS CAROL.

If you
Suspect it, call some witness of my vows,
I will contract myself.

FAIRFIELD.

And I am provided. –
Frank Tier, appear, and shew thy physnomy. –
He is a friend of mine, and you may trust him.

Trier comes forward.

MISTRESS CAROL.

What sum of money is it you would borrow?

TRIER.

I borrow?

MISTRESS CAROL.

This gentleman, your friend, has fully
Possessed me with your wants; nay, do not blush,
Debt is no sin: though my own monies, sir,
Are all abroad, yet, upon good security,

Which he answers you can put in, I will speak
To a friend of mine.

FAIRFIELD.
What security?

MISTRESS CAROL.
Yourselves, and two sufficient aldermen,
For men are mortal, and may break.

FAIRFIELD.
What mean you?

MISTRESS CAROL.
You shall have fifty pounds for forty weeks,
To do you a pleasure.

FAIRFIELD.
You'll not use me thus?

TRIER.
Fare you well;
You have miraculously brought things about.

Exit Trier.

MISTRESS CAROL.
You work by strategem and ambuscado.
Do you not think yourself a proper gentleman,
Whom by your want of hair some hold a wit too?
You know my heart, and every thought within it!
How I am caught! do I not melt like honey
I' the dog-days? Why do you look so staring?

FAIRFIELD.
Do you not love me for all this?

MISTRESS CAROL.
Would I had art enough to draw your picture,
It would show rarely at the Exchange; you have
A medley in your face of many nations:
Your nose is Roman, which your next debauchment
At tavern, with the help of pot or candlestick,
May turn to Indian, flat; your lip is Austrian,
And you do well to bite it; for your chin,
It does incline to the Bavarian poke,
But seven years may disguise it with a beard,
And make it – more ill favoured; you have eyes,
Especially when you goggle thus, not much
Unlike a Jew's, and yet some men might take 'em
For Turk's by the two half moons that rise about 'em. –
(*Aside.*) I am an infidel to use him thus.

FAIRFIELD.
Till now, I never was myself; farewell
For ever, woman, not worth love or anger.

MISTRESS CAROL.
Do you hear? one word. – (*Aside.*) I'd fain speak kindly to him
Why dost not rail at me?

FAIRFIELD.
No, I will laugh at thee, and at myself,
To have been so much a fool; you are a fine may game.

MISTRESS CAROL (*aside*).
I shall fool too much.
– But one word more;
By all the faith and love of womankind,
Believe me now – (*Aside.*) it will not out.

FAIRFIELD.
Farewell;
When next I doat upon thee, be a monster.

MISTRESS CAROL.
Hark, sir, the nightingale; there is better luck
Coming towards us.

FAIRFIELD.
When you are out of breath,
You will give over; and for better luck,
I do believe the bird, for I can leave thee,
And not be in love with my own torment.

MISTRESS CAROL.
How, sir?

FAIRFIELD.
I have said; stay you and practise with the bird,
'Twas Philomel, they say; an thou wert one,
I should new ravish thee.

Exit Fairfie

MISTRESS CAROL.
I must to the coach and weep, my heart will break else;
I'm glad he does not see me.

Exit Mistress Car

CT FOUR

ene One

nother part of the Park.
ter Lord Bonvile and Julietta.

LIETTA.
> Whither will you walk, my lord? you may engage
> Yourself too far, and lose your sport.

RD BONVILE.
> I would
> Go farther for a little sport; you mean
> The horse-race; they're not come into the Park yet,
> I might do something else, and return time
> Enough to w· ı five hundred pieces.

LIETTA.
> Your lordship had no fortune in the last match;
> I wished your confidence a happier success.

RD BONVILE.
> We must lose sometimes. – Hark the nightingale!

LIETTA.
> You win, my lord, I dare engage myself.

RD BONVILE.
> You make the omen fortunate; this bird
> Doth prophesy good luck.

LIETTA.
> 'Tis the first time I heard it.

RD BONVILE.
> And I, this spring; let's walk a little further.

LIETTA.
> I am not weary, but –

RD BONVILE.
> You may trust your person, lady.

LIETTA.
> I were too much wicked to suspect your honour,
> And in this place.

RD BONVILE.
> This place! the place were good enough,
> If you were bad enough, and as prepared

As I. There have been stories, that some have
Struck many deer within the Park.

JULIETTA.
> Foul play.
> If I did think your honour had a thought
> To venture at unlawful game, I should
> Have brought less confidence.

Enter Trier, at a distance.

LORD BONVILE.
> Ha! Trier?
> What, does he follow us?

JULIETTA.
> To show I dare
> Be bold upon your virtue, take no notice,
> I'll waft him back again; my lord, walk forward.

> > *Waves her hand, and exits with Lord Bonvile.*

TRIER.
> Thus far alone? yet why do I suspect?
> Hang jealousy, 'tis naught, it breeds too many
> Worms in our brains; and yet she might have suffered me –

Enter Lacy and Mistress Bonavent.

> Master Lacy, and his bride!

MISTRESS BONAVENT.
> I was wont to have one always in my chamber.

LACY.
> Thou shalt have a whole quire of nightingales.

MISTRESS BONAVENT.
> I heard it yesterday warble so prettily!

LACY.
> They say 'tis lucky, when it is the first
> Bird that salutes our ear.

MISTRESS BONAVENT.
> Do you believe it?

TRIER.
> I am of his mind, and love a happy augury.

LACY.
> Observe the first note always –

> (*Within*:) Cuckoo!

LACY.
> Is this the nightingale?

MISTRESS BONAVENT.
> Why do you look so?

LACY.
> Are not we married?
> I would not have been a bachelor to have heard it.

MISTRESS BONAVENT.
> To them they say 'tis fatal.

TRIER.
> And to married men
> Cuckoo is no delightful note; I shall
> Be superstitious.

MISTRESS BONAVENT.
> Let's walk a little further.

LACY.
> I wait upon thee.

> (*Again within.*) 'Cuckoo!'

LACY.
> Hark, still, ha, ha, ha!

> *Exeunt Mistress Bonavent and Lacy.*

TRIER.
> I am not much in love with the broad ditty.

> *Enter Fairfield.*

FAIRFIELD.
> Frank Trier, I have been seeking thee
> About the Park.

TRIER.
> What to do?

FAIRFIELD.
> To be merry for half an hour; I find
> A scurvy melancholy creep upon me,
> I'll try what sack will do; I have sent my footman
> To the Maurice for a bottle, we shall meet him.
> I'll tell thee t'other story of my lady.

TRIER.
> I'll wait on you.

FAIRFIELD.
> But that she is my sister,
> I'd have thee forswear women; but let's walk.

> *Exeunt.*

Scene Two

The same.
Enter Bonavent.

BONAVENT.
> This way they marched; I hope they will not leap
> The pale; I do not know the disposition
> Of my capering gentleman, and therefore 'twill not
> Be indiscretion to observe him; things
> Must be a little better reconciled. –
> The nightingale! – this can presage no hurt,
> But I shall lose my pigeons; – they are in view,
> Fair and far off.

> *Exit Bonave*

Scene Three

Another part of the same.
Enter Venture and Rider.

VENTURE.
> He must be a Pegasus that beats me.

RIDER.
> Yet your confidence may deceive you; you will ride
> Against a jockey, that has horsemanship.

VENTURE.
> A jockey! a jackanapes on horseback rather;
> A monkey or a masty dog would show
> A giant to him; an I were Alexander,
> I would lay the world upon my mare; she shall
> Run with the devil for a hundred pieces,
> Make the match who will.

RIDER.
> Not I, you shall excuse me,
> Nor would I win his money.

VENTURE.
> Whose?

RIDER.
> The devil's;
> My gold has burnt this twelve months in my pocket;
> A little of his amongst, would scorch my thighs,
> And make such tinder of my linings, that
> My breeches never after would hold money;

But let this pass; where's Lacy and his bride?

NTURE.
They are walked to hear the nightingale.

ΟΕR.
The nightingale! I have not heard one this year.

NTURE.
Listen, and we shall hear one presently.

(*Within:*) – Cuckoo!

NTURE.
The bird speaks to you.

ΟΕR.
No, 'tis to you.

NTURE.
Now do I suspect
I shall lose the race.

ΟΕR.
Despair for a cuckoo!

NTURE.
A cuckoo will not flatter,
His word will go before a gentleman's,
In the city; 'tis an understanding bird,
And seldom fails; a cuckoo! I'll hedge in
My money presently.

ΟΕR.
For shame, be confident.

NTURE.
Will you go half?

ΟΕR.
I'll go it all, or any thing.

NTURE.
Hang cuckoos then.

Enter Lord Bonvile, Julietta, Lacy, and Mistress Bonavent.

RD BONVILE.
How now, gentlemen?

NTURE.
Your honour's servants.

ΟΕR.
Ladies, I kiss your hands.

LORD BONVILE.
You are the man will run away with all
The gold anon.

VENTURE.
Your jockey must fly else.

RIDER.
I'll hold your honour thirty pieces more.

LORD BONVILE.
'Tis done.

JULIETTA.
Do you ride yourself?

VENTURE.
I shall have the reins in my own hand, lady.

MISTRESS BONAVENT.
Master Rider, saw you not my cousin?

Enter Mistress Carol.

Cry mercy, she is here. – I thought you'd followed us.

LORD BONVILE.
Your kinswoman? –
I shall be honoured to be your servant, lady.

MISTRESS CAROL.
Alas, my lord, you'll lose by't!

LORD BONVILE.
What?

MISTRESS CAROL.
Honour, by being my servant; here's a brace
Of gentlemen will tell you as much.

VENTURE.
But will
Say nothing, for our credits.

MISTRESS BONAVENT.
You look as you had wept.

MISTRESS CAROL.
I weep! For what?
Come towards the lodge, and drink a syllabub.

MISTRESS BONAVENT.
A match!

LACY.
As we walk, Jack Venture, thou shalt sing
The song thou mad'st o' the horses.

VENTURE.
> You shall pardon me.

RIDER.
> What, among friends? my lord, if you'd speak to him.

LORD BONVILE.
> A song by all means,
> Prithee let me entreat it; what's the subject?

LACY.
> Of all the running horses.

VENTURE.
> Horses and mares, put them together.

LORD BONVILE.
> Let's have it; come, I hear you can sing rarely,

RIDER.
> An excellent voice.

LACY.
> A ravishing tone.

VENTURE.
> 'Tis a very ballad, my lord, and a coarse tune.

LORD BONVILE.
> The better; why, does any tune become
> A gentleman so well as a ballad? hang
> Curiosity in music; leave those crotchets
> To men that get their living with a song. –
> Come, come, begin.

Venture sings.

SONG.
> Come, Muses all, that dwell nigh the fountain.
> Made by the wingèd horse's heel,
> Which firked with his rider over each mountain,
> Let me your galloping raptures feel.
> > I do not sing of fleas, or frogs,
> > Nor of the well-mouthed hunting dogs.
> Let me be just, all praises must
> Be given to well-breathed Jilian Thrust.
>
> Young Constable and Kill Deer's famous,
> The Cat, the Mouse, and Neddy Gray;
> With nimble Peggybrig, you cannot shame us
> With Spaniard nor with Spinola.
> > Hill-climbing White Rose praise doth not lack,
> > Handsome Dunbar, and Yellow Jack;
> But if I be just, all praises must

> Be given to well-breathed Jilian Thrust.
>
> Sure-spurred Sloven, true-running Robin,
> Of Young Shaver I do not say less,
> Strawberry Soam, and let Spider pop in,
> Fine Brackly, and brave Lurching Bess.
> > Victorious too was Herring Shotten,
> > And Spit-in's-arse is not forgotten;
> But if I be just, all honour must
> Be given to well-breathed Jilian Thrust.
>
> Lusty George, and, gentlemen, hark yet,
> To winning Mackarel, fine-mouthed Freak,
> Bay Tarrall, that won the cup at Newmarket,
> Thundering Tempest, Black Dragon eke.
> > Precious Sweet Lips, I do not lose,
> > Nor Toby with his golden shoes;
> But if I be just, all honour must
> Be given to well-breathed Jilian Thrust.

LORD BONVILE.
> Excellent! how think you, lady?

JULIETTA.
> I like it very well.

MISTRESS CAROL.
> I never thought you were a poet, sir.

VENTURE.
> No, no, I do but dabble.

MISTRESS CAROL.
> You can sing rarely too; how were these parts
> Unobserved, invisible?

VENTURE.
> You may see, lady.

JULIETTA.
> Good sir, your pardon.

VENTURE.
> Do you love singing? hum; la, la (*Sings.*)

MISTRESS CAROL.
> Who would have thought these qualities were in you?

VENTURE.
> Now or never.

MISTRESS CAROL.
> Why, I was cozened.

NTURE.
    You are not the first I have cozened; shall I wash
    Your faces with the drops of Helicon?
    I have fancies in my head.

STRESS CAROL.
    Like Jupiter, you want a Vulcan but
    To cleave your skull, and out peeps bright Minerva.

LIETTA.
    When you return I'll tell you more, my lord.

NTURE.
    Give me a subject.

STRESS BONAVENT.
    Prithee coz, do.

STRESS CAROL.
    Let it be – How much you dare suffer for me.

NTURE.
    Enough – hum, fa, la, la.

Enter Page.

GE.
    Master Venture, you are expected.

RD BONVILE.
    Are they come?

GE.
    This half hour, my lord.

RD BONVILE.
    I must see the mare: you will excuse this rudeness. –
    Sirrah, stay you, and wait upon these ladies.

                            Exit Lord Bonvile.

NTURE.
    'Tis time to make me ready. –
    Ladies, I take this leave in prose,
    You shall see me next in other feet.

                            Exit Venture.

DER.
    I wish your syllabub were nectar, lady.

STRESS BONAVENT.
    We thank you, sir, and here it comes already.

Enter Milkmaid with a bowl.

JULIETTA.
    So, so; is it good milk?

MISTRESS BONAVENT.
    Of a red cow?

MISTRESS CAROL.
    You talk as you inclined to a consumption;
    Is the wine good?

MILKMAID.
    It comes from his Excellence' head.

MISTRESS CAROL.
    My service to you, lady, and to him
    Your thoughts prefer.

MISTRESS BONAVENT.
    A health!

MISTRESS CAROL.
    No deep one; 'tis lawful for gentlewomen
    To wish well to their friends.

JULIETTA.
    You have obliged me – the wishes of all happiness
    To him your heart hath chosen!

MISTRESS BONAVENT.
    Duty now
    Requires I should be willing to receive it:
    As many joys to you both, when you are married!

MISTRESS CAROL.
    Married?

JULIETTA.
    You have not vowed to die a virgin,
    I know an humble servant of your's, lady.

MISTRESS CAROL.
    Mine!

JULIETTA.
    Would be sorry you should be a nun.

MISTRESS CAROL.
    Do you think he loves me, then?

JULIETTA.
    I do not think
    He can dissemble where he does profess
    Affection; I know his heart by mine:
    Fairfield is my brother!

MISTRESS CAROL.
Your brother? then the danger's not so great;
But let us change our argument. With your pardon,
Come hither, pretty one; how old are you?

PAGE.
I am young, lady;
I hope you do not take me for a dwarf.

MISTRESS BONAVENT.
How young, I pray then?

PAGE.
Four summers since my life was questioned,
And then a jury of years did pass upon me.

MISTRESS CAROL.
He is upon the matter, then, fifteen.

PAGE.
A game at noddy.

MISTRESS CAROL.
You can play your cards already, it seems:
Come, drink of this syllabub.

PAGE.
I shall spoil your game, ladies;
For if there be sack in it, it may make
You flush a three.

JULIETTA.
The boy would seem witty.

PAGE.
I hope, ladies, you will pardon me; my lord commanded me to
wait upon you, and I can do you no better service than to make
you laugh.

Enter Fairfield and Trier.

TRIER.
They're here, bless you!

MISTRESS BONAVENT.
Master Fairfield, you are welcome.

FAIRFIELD.
I presume so, but howsoever it skills not.

TRIER.
I do not come to borrow money.

MISTRESS CAROL.
And yet all they that do so are no fools;
Money or lands make not a man the wiser,

I know handsome gentlemen have pawned their clothes.

TRIER.
I'll pawn my skin too, with a woman.

MISTRESS CAROL.
Wipe your mouth; here's to you, sir!

TRIER.
I'll pledge you, quicksilver. Where is your lord?

PAGE.
He has left Virgo, sir, to go to Libra,
To see the horsemen weighed.

TRIER.
Lady, my service!

JULIETTA.
Brother, you interpose too far; my lord
Has me honourably, and I must tell you,
Somebody has made a fault.

MISTRESS BONAVENT.
Master Fairfield!

FAIRFIELD.
I kiss your hand.

TRIER.
My lord and you have walked.

JULIETTA.
Yes, sir.

FAIRFIELD.
My sister shall excuse; here's to thee and thy cream bowl.

MILKMAID.
I thank your worship.

FAIRFIELD.
There is more honesty in thy petticoat,
Than twenty satin ones.

MISTRESS BONAVENT.
Do you know that?

FAIRFIELD.
I know by her pail; an she were otherwise,
T'would turn her milk. – Come hither, let me kiss thee.

Kisses the Milkmaid.

Now I am confirmed, he that shall marry thee
Shall take thee a virgin at my peril.

MISTRESS BONAVENT.
Have you such skill in maidenheads?

FAIRFIELD.
I'll know't by a kiss,
Better than any doctor by her urine. –
Be merry with thy cow, farewell! – Come, Frank:
That wit and good clothes should infect a woman!

JULIETTA.
I'll tell you more hereafter; pray let's hear
Who wins.

TRIER.
Your servant, ladies.

Exeunt Fairfield and Trier.

Enter Jockey and Gentlemen.

FIRST GENTLEMAN.
What dost think, Jockey?

2D GENTLEMAN.
The crack o' the field's against you.

JOCKEY.
Let 'em crack nuts.

FIRST GENTLEMAN.
What weight?

2D GENTLEMAN.
I think he has the heels.

3D GENTLEMAN.
Get but the start.

JOCKEY.
However, if I get within his quarters
Let him alone.

3D GENTLEMAN.
Montez à cheval.

Exeunt.

Confused noise of betting within, after that a shout.

MISTRESS CAROL.
They are started.

Re-enter Lord Bonvile, Rider, Trier and Fairfield.

RIDER.
Twenty pounds to fifteen!

LORD BONVILE.
'Tis done wi' ye!

FAIRFIELD.
Forty pounds to thirty!

LORD BONVILE.
Done! done! I'll take all odds.

TRIER.
My lord, I hold as much.

LORD BONVILE.
Not so.

TRIER.
Forty pounds to twenty.

LORD BONVILE.
Done, done!

Re-enter Lacy.

LACY.
You have lost all, my lord, an it were a million.

LORD BONVILE.
In your imagination; who can help it?

LACY.
Venture had the start, and keeps it.

LORD BONVILE.
Gentlemen, you have a fine time to triumph,
'Tis not your odds that makes you win.

(*Within:*) Venture! Venture!

Exeunt all but the ladies.

JULIETTA.
Shall we venture nothing o' the horses?
What odds against my lord!

MISTRESS CAROL.
Silk stockings.

JULIETTA.
To a pair of perfumed gloves? I take it.

MISTRESS CAROL.
Done!

MISTRESS BONAVENT.
And I as much.

JULIETTA.
Done, with you both!

MISTRESS CAROL.
I'l have 'em Spanish scent.

JULIETTA.
    The stockings shall be scarlet; if you choose
    Your scent, I'll choose my colour.

MISTRESS CAROL.
    'Tis done; if Venture
    Knew but my lay, it would half break his neck now.

A shout within, and cry of A Jockey!

JULIETTA.
    Ha! is the wind in that coast? hark! the noise
    Is jockey now.

MISTRESS CAROL.
    'Tis but a pair of gloves.

    (*Within:*) A jockey!

JULIETTA.
    Still it holds. –

Re-enter Lord Bonvile.

    How have you sped, my lord?

LORD BONVILE.
    Won, won! I knew by instinct
    The mare would put some trick upon him.

MISTRESS BONAVENT.
    Then we have lost; but, good my lord, the circumstance.

LORD BONVILE.
    Great John-at-all-adventure, and grave Jockey.
    Mounted their several mares. – I shall not tell
    The story out for laughing, ha, ha ha! –
    But this in brief – Jockey was left behind,
    The pity and the scorn of all; the odds
    Played 'bout my ears like cannon, but less dangerous.
    I took all still, the acclamations were
    For Venture, whose disdainful mare threw dirt
    In my old Jockey's face, all hopes forsaking us,
    Two hundred pieces desperate, and two thousand
    Oaths sent after them, upon the sudden,
    When we expected no such trick, we saw
    My rider, that was domineering ripe,
    Vault o'er his mare into a tender slough,
    Where he was much beholding to one shoulder,
    For saving of his neck; his beast recovered,
    And he by this time somewhat mortified,
    Besides mortarified, hath left the triumph
    To his Olympic adversary, who shall
    Ride hither in full pomp on his Bucephalus,

With his victorious bagpipe.

MISTRESS CAROL.
    I would fain see
    How Venture looks.

LORD BONVILE.
    He's here; ha, ha!

Enter Venture, covered with mud, and Rider.

VENTURE.
    I told you as much before;
    You would not believe the cuckoo.

MISTRESS CAROL.
    Why, how now, sir?

VENTURE.
    An' I had broke my neck in a clean way,
    'Twould ne'er have grieved me. – Lady, I am your's;
    Thus Caesar fell.

LORD BONVILE.
    Not in a slough, dear Jack.

VENTURE.
    You shall hear further from me.

RIDER.
    Come to Knightsbridge.

VENTURE.
    That cuckoo was a witch, I'll take my death on't.

Exit Ventu

LORD BONVILE.
    Here comes the conqueror.

*Enter a Bagpiper, and Jockey in triumph, followed by Bonave
Trier, and Fairfield.*

    'Lo, from the conquest of Jerusalem
    Returns Vespasian!' – Ha, ha! mer – mercy, Jockey.

JOCKEY.
    I told you, if I came within his quarters.

ALL.
    A jockey, a jockey!

    *Exeunt all but Lacy, his Bride, and Mistress Car
Re-enter Bonavent and Bagpiper.*

BONAVENT.
    This shall be but your earnest; (*Gives him money.*) – follow m

At pretty distance, and when I say 'draw,'
Play me a galliard. – By your favour, sir,
Shall I speak a cool word with you?

CY.

With all my heart.

NAVENT.

You do owe me a dance, if you remember,
And I will have it now; no dispute. – Draw!

Bagpiper plays. Lacy draws his sword.

That will not serve your turn; come, shake your heels,
You hear a tune; I will not change my tool
For a case of rapiers; keep off, at your perils,
I have sworn.

STRESS BONAVENT.

For Heaven's sake some to part 'em.

CY.

Dost hear?

NAVENT.

And you may hear the bagpipe is not dumb:
Will you to this gear? or do you mean to try

Draws his sword.

How this will scower you? Come, come, I will have it.

CY.

Hold! I will.

He dances, meantime enter Lord Bonvile and Trier.

NAVENT.

So; now we are on equal terms, and if
You like it or not, I'll use my t'other instrument.

CY.

Thou art a brave fellow; come your ways.

RD BONVILE.

Hold!
You shall not fight, I'll understand your quarrel.

CY.

Good my lord.
Let's have one pass.

STRESS BONAVENT.

Your weapons shall run through me;
And I must tell you, sir, you have been injurious –

BONAVENT.

Good lady, why? in doing myself right?

MISTRESS BONAVENT.

In wronging me.

BONAVENT.

I am not sensible of that.

MISTRESS BONAVENT.

Could any shame be fastened upon him,
Wherein I have no share?

BONAVENT.

I was provoked
By him, if you remember, and was not
Born so unequal to him, I should suffer
His poor affront.

MISTRESS BONAVENT.

This was a day of peace,
The day wherein the holy priest hath tied
Our hearts together; Hymen's tapers yet
Are burning, and it cannot be a sin
Less than a sacrilege, to extinguish them
With blood, and in contempt of Heaven's proceeding,
Thus to conspire our separation.
No Christian would profane the marriage day:
And when all other wish us joys, could you
Intrude yourself to poison all our mirth,
Blast, in the very budding, all our happiness
Our hopes had laid up for us?

BONAVENT.

I was a stranger.

MISTRESS BONAVENT.

That makes your more uncivil; we were merry,
Which could not offend you.

BONAVENT.

I had no thought
To violate your mirth.

MISTRESS BONAVENT.

What came you for?
With whom had you acquaintance? or what favour
Gave you access, at so unfit a time,
To interrupt our calm and free delights?
You cannot plead any abuse, where you
Were never known, that should incite you to
Revenge it there: I take it you were never
His rival.

BONAVENT.
    'Tis confessed.

MISTRESS BONAVENT.
    What malice then
    Prevailed above your reason to pursue us
    With this injustice?

BONAVENT.
    Lady, give me leave.
    I were a villain to be guilty of
    The baseness you accuse me: your servant
    Shall quit me from intrusion, and my soul
    Is my best witness, that I brought no malice
    But unstained thoughts into your roof; but when
    I was made the common laughter, I had been
    Less than a man, to think of no return,
    And had he been the only of my blood,
    I would not be so much the shame of soldier,
    To have been tamed, and suffered; and you are
    Too hasty in your judgment; I could say more,
    But 'tis dishonour to expostulate
    These causes with a woman: I had reason
    To call him to account, you know not all
    My provocation; things are not with me
    As with another man.

MISTRESS BONAVENT (*aside*).
    How is that? the matter
    May spread too far; some former quarrel, – 'tis
    My best to reconcile 'em. – Sir, I may
    Be ignorant; if anything have passed
    Before this morning, I pray pardon me;
    But as you are a gentleman, let me
    Prevail, your differences may here conclude;
    'Las, I am part of him now, and between
    A widow and his wife, if I be thus
    Divorced –

BONAVENT.
    I'll be his servant.

MISTRESS BONAVENT.
    Sir, you show
    A noble disposition. – Good my lord,
    Compose their differences. – Prithee meet his friendship.

BONAVENT.
    I have satisfaction, and desire his love.

LACY.
    Thou hast done but like a gentleman; thy hand,

I'll love thee while I live.

LORD BONVILE.
    Why so; all friends.

BONAVENT.
    I meet it with a heart; and for disturbing
    Your mirth today –

LACY.
    No, no disturbance.

BONAVENT.
    Then give me but the favour
    To show I wish no sorrow to the bride:
    I have a small oblation, which she must
    Accept, or I shall doubt we are not friends;
    'Tis all I have to offer at your wedding.

    Gives Mistress Bonavent a paper.

MISTRESS BONAVENT.
    Ha!

BONAVENT.
    There's my hand
    To justify it at fit time. – Peruse it,
    My lord, I shall be studious
    How to deserve your favour.

LORD BONVILE.
    I am yours.

LACY.
    My lord, let me obtain you'll honour me
    To-night.

MISTRESS BONAVENT (*walks aside with the paper, and reads*). 'I w
    taken by a Turkish pirate, and detained many years a prison
    in an island, where I had died his captive, had not a worth
    merchant thence redeemed and furnished me.' –
    Blessed delivery!

    Enter a Servant and delivers a letter to Mistress Carol.

MISTRESS CAROL.
    To me! from Venture? he is very mindful;

    Reads.

    Good, I shall make use of this.

MISTRESS BONAVENT (*reading*).
    – 'Til then conceal me.'

MISTRESS CAROL.
    Excellent stuff,
    But I must have another name subscribed.

LORD BONVILE.
    Will you walk, ladies? (*Gives money to the Park-keepers.*)

MISTRESS CAROL.
    Your servants wait upon you.

KEEPERS.
    We humbly thank your honour.

2D KEEPER.
    A brave spark.

1T KEEPER.
    Spark! he's the very Bonfire of nobility.

                         Exeunt.

ACT FIVE

Scene One

A room in Bonavent's House.
Enter Lacy, Mistress Bonavent, Lord Bonvile, Julietta, Mistress Carol, and Trier.

LACY.
    My lord, you honour us.

MISTRESS BONAVENT.
    And what we want
    In honourable entertainment, we beseech
    Our duties may supply in your construction.

LORD BONVILE.
    What needs this ceremony?

LACY.
    Thou art welcome, too, Frank Trier.

TRIER.
    I give you thanks, and wish you still more joy, sir.

MISTRESS BONAVENT.
    We'll show your lordship a poor gallery.

LACY.
    But, where's my new acquaintance?

MISTRESS BONAVENT.
    His nag outstripped the coaches,
    He'll be your guest anon, fear not!

    Exeunt all but Mistress Carol and Julietta.

MISTRESS CAROL.
    While they
    Compliment with my lord, let you and I
    Change a few words.

JULIETTA.
    As many as you please.

MISTRESS CAROL.
    Then to the purpose. Touching your brother, lady,
    'Twere tedious to repeat he has been pleased
    To think well of me; and to trouble you
    With the discourse how I have answered it,
    'Twere vain; but thus – howe'er he seem to carry it
    While you were present, I do find him desperate.

JULIETTA.
How!

MISTRESS CAROL.
Nay, I speak no conjecture;
I have more intelligence than you imagine.
You are his sister,
And nature binds you to affect his safety.
By some convenient messenger send for him;
But, as you love his life, do not delay it:
Alas, I shall be sorry any gentleman
Should, for my sake, take any desperate course.

JULIETTA.
But are you serious?

MISTRESS CAROL.
Perhaps good counsel
Applied while his despair is green, may cure him,
If not –

JULIETTA.
You make me wonder.

MISTRESS CAROL.
I know the inconsiderate will blame
Me for his death; I shall be railed upon,
And have a thousand cruelties thrown on me;
But would you have me promise love, and flatter him?
I would do much to save his life: I could
Show you a paper that would make you bleed
To see his resolution, and what
Strange and unimitable ways he has
Vowed to pursue; I tremble to think on 'em.
There's not a punishment in fiction,
(And poets write enough of hell, if you
Have read their story,) but he'll try the worst.
Were it not that I fear him every minute,
And that all haste were requisite to save him,
You should peruse his letter.

JULIETTA.
Letter! Since
We saw him?

MISTRESS CAROL.
Since; I must confess I wondered,
But you in this shall see I have no malice.
I pray send for him; as I am a gentlewoman,
I have pure intention to preserve his life;
And 'cause I see the truth of his affliction,
Which may be your's, or mine, or anybody's,

Whose passions are neglected, I will try
My best skill to reduce him. Here's Master Trier.

Re-entr Trier.

He now depends upon your charity;
Send for him, by the love you bear a brother.

TRIER.
Will you not chide my want of manners, gentlewomen,
To interrupt your dialogue?

JULIETTA.
We have done, sir.

MISTRESS CAROL.
I shall be still your servant.

JULIETTA.
Here's a riddle;
But I will do't –
Shall I presume upon you for a favour?

Re-enter Lord Bonvile.

TRIER.
You shall impose on me a greater trouble.
My lord!

JULIETTA.
Your ear. (*Whispers to Trier.*)

LORD BONVILE.
We miss you above, lady.

JULIETTA.
My lord, I wait upon you; I beseech
Your pardon but a minute. – Will you do this?
It is an office he may thank you for,
Beside my acknowledgment.

TRIER.
Yes, I'll go, –
(*Aside.*) And yet I do not like to be sent off,
This is the second time.

Exit Tri

JULIETTA.
Now I am for your lordship. What's your pleasure?

LORD BONVILE.
I would be your echo, lady, and return
Your last word – pleasure.

JULIETTA.
May you never want it!

LORD BONVILE.
    This will not serve my turn.

JULIETTA.
    What, my lord?

LORD BONVILE.
    This is the charity of some rich men,
    That, passing by some monument that stoops
    With age, whose ruins plead for a repair,
    Pity the fall of such a goodly pile,
    But will not spare from their superfluous wealth,
    To be the benefactor.

JULIETTA.
    I acknowledge
    That empty wishes are their shame, that have
    Ability to do a noble work,
    And fly the action.

LORD BONVILE.
    Come, you may apply it.
    I would not have you a gentlewoman of your word
    Alone, they're deeds that crown all; what you wish me,
    Is in your own ability to give;
    You understand me: will you at length consent
    To multiply? we'll 'point a place and time,
    And all the world shall envy us.

JULIETTA.
    My lord!

LORD BONVILE.
    Lord me no lords; shall we join lips upon't?
    Why do you look as you still wondered at me?
    Do I not make a reasonable motion?
    Is't only in myself? shall not you share
    I' the delight? or do I appear a monster
    'Bove all mankind, you shun my embraces thus?
    There be some ladies in the world have drawn
    Cuts for me; I have been talked on and commended,
    Howe'er you please to value me.

JULIETTA.
    Did they
    See you thus perfectly?

LORD BONVILE.
    Not always; 'twas
    Sometimes a little darker, when they praised me.
    I have the same activity.

JULIETTA.
    You are
    Something – I would not name, my lord.

LORD BONVILE.
    And yet you do; you call me lord, that's something,
    And you consider all men are not born to't.

JULIETTA.
    'Twere better not to have been born to honours,
    Than forfeit them so poorly; he is truly
    Noble, and then best justifies his blood,
    When he can number the descents of virtue.

LORD BONVILE.
    You'll not degrade me?

JULIETTA.
    'Tis not in my power,
    Or will, my lord, and yet you press me strangely.
    As you are a person, separate and distinct,
    By your high blood, above me and my fortunes,
    Thus low I bend; you have no noble title
    Which I not bow to, they are characters
    Which we should read at distance, and there is
    Not one that shall with more devotion
    And honour of your birth, express her service:
    It is my duty, where the king has sealed
    His favours, I should show humility,
    My best obedience, to his act.

LORD BONVILE.
    So should
    All handsome women, that will be good subjects.

JULIETTA.
    But if to all those honourable names,
    That marked you for the people's reverence,
    In such a vicious age, you dare rise up
    Example too of goodness, they which teach
    Their knees a compliment, will give their heart;
    And I among the number of the humblest,
    Most proud to serve your lordship, and would refuse
    No office or command, that should engage me
    To any noble trial; this addition
    Of virtue is above all shine of state,
    And will draw more admirers: but I must
    Be bold to tell you, sir, unless you prove
    A friend to virtue, were your honour centupled,
    Could you pile titles till you reach the clouds,
    Were every petty manor you possess

A kingdom, and the blood of many princes
United in your veins, with these had you
A person that had more attraction
Than poesy can furnish, love withal.
Yet I, I in such infinite distance, am
As much above you in my innocence.

LORD BONVILE.
This becomes not.

JULIETTA.
'Tis the first liberty
I ever took to speak myself; I have
Been bold in the comparison, but find not
Wherein I have wronged virtue, pleading for it,

LORD BONVILE.
How long will you continue thus?

JULIETTA.
I wish
To have my last hour witness of these thoughts;
And I will hope, before that time, to hear
Your lordship of another mind.

LORD BONVILE.
I know not,
'Tis time enough to think o' that hereafter:
I'll be a convertite within these two days,
Upon condition you and I may have
One bout to-night; nobody hears.

JULIETTA.
Alas!
You plunge too far, and are within this minute,
Further from Heaven than ever.

LORD BONVILE.
I may live to
Requite the courtesy.

JULIETTA.
Live, my lord, to be
Your country's honour and support, and think not
Of these poor dreams.

LORD BONVILE.
I find not
Desire to sleep; – an I were abed with you –

JULIETTA.
'Tis not improbable, my lord, but you
May live to be an old man, and fill up

A seat among the grave nobility;
When your cold blood shall starve your wanton thoughts,
And your slow pulse beat like your body's knell,
When time hath snowed upon your hair, oh then
Will it be any comfort to remember
The sins of your wild youth? how many wives
Or virgins you have dishonoured? in their number,
Would any memory of me (should I
Be sinful to consent), not fetch a tear
From you, perhaps a sigh, to break your heart?
Will you not wish then you had never mixed
With atheists, and those men whose wits are vented
In oaths and blasphemy, (now the pride of gentlemen,)
That strike at Heaven, and make a game of thunder?

LORD BONVILE (*aside*).
If this be true, what a wretched thing should I
Appear now, if I were any thing but a lord?
I do not like myself. –
Give me thy hand; since there's no remedy,
Be honest! – there's no harm in this, I hope.
I will not tell thee all my mind at once;
If I do turn Carthusian, and renounce
Flesh upon this, the devil is like to have
The worst on't. But I am expected.

Exit Bonv

JULIETTA.
My lord, I'll follow you. –

Enter Fairfield and Trier.

Brother, welcome! –
Sir, we are both obliged to you.
A friend of your's desires some private conference.

FAIRFIELD.
With me?

JULIETTA (*aside*). He does not look so desperate. –
How do you, brother?

FAIRFIELD.
Well: – dost not see me? –

JULIETTA.
I'll come to you presently.

E

FAIRFIELD.
What's the meaning?

TRIER.

    Nay, I know not;
She is full of mysteries of late.

Re-enter Julietta with Mistress Carol.

    She's here again; there is some trick in it.

JULIETTA.

    Brother, I sent for you, and I think 'twas time;
Pray hearken to this gentlewoman, she will
Give you good counsel. – You and I withdraw, sir.

TRIER.

    Whither you please.

Exeunt Julietta and Trier.

MISTRESS CAROL.

    You are a strange gentleman;
Alas! what do you mean? is it because
I have dealt justly with you, without flattery
Told you my heart, you'll take these wicked courses?
But I am loath to chide, yet I must tell you,
You are to blame; alas! you know affection
Is not to be compelled; I have been as kind
To you as other men, nay, I still thought
A little better of you, and will you
Give such example to the rest?
Because, forsooth, I do not love you, will you
Be desperate?

FAIRFIELD.

    Will I be desperate?

MISTRESS CAROL.

    'Twere a fine credit for you, but perhaps
You'll go to hell to be revenged on me,
And teach the other gentlemen to follow you,
That men may say, 'twas long of me, and rail at
My unkindness; is this all your Christianity?
Or could you not prosecute your impious purpose,
But you must send me word on't, and perplex
My conscience with your devilish devices?
Is this a letter to be sent a mistress?

FAIRFIELD.

    I send a letter?

MISTRESS CAROL (*gives him the letter*).

    You were best deny your hand.

FAIRFIELD.

    My name subscribed! who has done this? – (*Reads.*)
      'Rivers of hell, I come; Charon, thy oar
      Is needless, I will swim unto the shore,
      And beg of Pluto, and of Proserpine,
      That all the damnèd torments may be mine;
      With Tantalus I'll stand up to the chin
      In waves; upon Ixion's wheel I'll spin
      The sister's thread; quail Cerberus with my groan,
      And take no physic for the rolling stone:
      I'll drown myself a hundred times a day –'

MISTRESS CAROL.

    There be short days in hell.

FAIRFIELD.

      'And burn myself as often, if you say
      The word. –'

MISTRESS CAROL.

    Alas! not I.

FAIRFIELD.

      'And if I ever chance to come
      Within the confines of Elysium,
      The amazèd ghosts shall be aghast to see,
      How I will hang myself on every tree,
             Your's, till his neck be broke, Fairfield.'

    Here's a strange resolution!

MISTRESS CAROL.

    Is it not?
Whither is fled your piety? but, sir,
I have no meaning to exasperate
Thoughts that oppose your safety, and to show
I have compassion, and delight in no
Man's ruin, I will frame myself to love you.

FAIRFIELD.

    Will you? why, thank you.

MISTRESS CAROL.

    Here's my hand, I will;
Be comforted; I have a stronger faith.

FAIRFIELD.

    I see then you have charity for a need.

MISTRESS CAROL.

    I'll lose my humour to preserve a life.
You might have met with some hard-hearted mistress,
That would have suffered you to hang or drown
Yourself.

FAIRFIELD.
> I might indeed.

MISTRESS CAROL.
> And carried news
> To the distressed ghosts; but I am merciful:
> But do not you mistake me, for I do not
> This out of any extraordinary
> Former good will, only to save your life.
> There be so many beams convenient,
> And you may slip out of the world before
> We are aware; beside, you dwell too near
> The river; if you should be melancholy,
> After some tides, you would come in, and be
> More talked off than the pilchards; but I have done.
> You shall go to hell for me: I now
> Am very serious, and if you please
> To think well of me, instantly we'll marry;
> I'll see how I can love you afterward.
> Shall we to the priest?

FAIRFIELD.
> By your good favour, no;
> I am in no such tune.

MISTRESS CAROL.
> You do suspect
> I jeer still: by my troth, I am in earnest.

FAIRFIELD.
> To save my life, you are content to marry me?

MISTRESS CAROL.
> Yes.

FAIRFIELD.
> To save thy life, I'll not be troubled with thee.

MISTRESS CAROL.
> How?

FAIRFIELD.
> No, madam jeer-all, I am now resolved:
> Talk, and talk out thy heart, I will not lose
> Myself a scruple; have you no more letters?
> They're pretty mirth; would I knew who subscribed
> My name! I am so far from hanging of myself,
> That I will live yet to be thy tormentor.
> Virtue, I thank thee for't! and for the more
> Security, I'll never doat again;
> Nor marry, nor endure the imagination
> Of your frail sex: this very night I will

> Be fitted for you all; I'll geld myself,
> 'Tis something less than hanging; and when I
> Have carved away all my concupiscence,
> Observe but how I'll triumph; nay, I'll do it,
> An there were no more men in the world.

Going.

MISTRESS CAROL.
> Sir, sir! as you love goodness, –
> I'll tell you all; first hear me, and then execute;
> You will not be so foolish; I do love you.

FAIRFIELD.
> I hope so, that I may revenge thy peevishness.

MISTRESS CAROL.
> My heart is full, and modesty forbids.
> I should use so many words; I see my folly,
> You may be just, and use me with like cruelty,
> But if you do, I can instruct myself,
> And be as miserable in deed as I
> Made you in supposition: my thoughts
> Point on no sensuality; remit
> What's past, and I will meet your best affection.
> I know you love me still; do not refuse me.

FAIRFIELD.
> I am as ticklish.

MISTRESS CAROL.
> Then, let's clap it up wisely,
> While we are both i' the humour; I do find
> A grudging, and your last words stick in my stomach.
> Say, is't a match? speak quickly, or for ever
> Hereafter hold your peace.

FAIRFIELD.
> Done!

MISTRESS CAROL.
> Why, done!

FAIRFIELD.
> Seal and deliver.

MISTRESS CAROL.
> My hand and heart; this shall suffice till morning.

FAIRFIELD.
> Each other's now by conquest, come let's to 'em.
> If you should fail now! –

MISTRESS CAROL.
 Hold me not worth the hanging.

Exeunt.

Scene Two

Another Room in the same.
Enter Julietta, Lord Bonvile, and Trier.

LORD BONVILE.
 I knew not
 She was thy mistress, which encouraged
 All my discourses.

TRIER.
 My lord, you have richly satisfied me, and
 Now I dare write myself the happiest lover
 In all the world. Know lady, I have tried you.

JULIETTA.
 You have, it seems!

TRIER.
 And I have found thee right
 And perfect gold, nor will I change thee for
 A crown imperial.

JULIETTA.
 And I have tried you,
 And found you cross; nor do I love my heart
 So ill, to change it with you.

TRIER.
 How's this?

JULIETTA.
 Unworthily you have suspected me,
 And cherished that bad humour, for which I know
 You never must have hope to gain my love.
 He that shall doubt my virtue, out of fancy,
 Merits my just suspicion and disdain.

LORD BONVILE.
 Oh fie, Frank, practise jealousy so soon!
 Distrust the truth of her thou lov'st! suspect
 Thy own heart sooner. – What I have said I have
 Thy pardon for; thou wert a wife for him
 Whose thoughts were ne'er corrupted.

TRIER.
 'Twas but a trial, and may plead for pardon.

JULIETTA.
 I pray deny me not that liberty:
 I will have proof, too, of the man I choose
 My husband; and believe me, if men be
 At such a loss of goodness, I will value
 Myself, and think no honour equal to
 Remain a virgin.

TRIER.
 I have made a trespass,
 Which if I cannot expiate, yet let me
 Dwell in your charity.

JULIETTA.
 You shall not doubt that. –

 Enter Fairfield, Mistress Carol, Lacy, and Mistress Bonavent.

 Pray, my lord, know him for your servant.

FAIRFIELD.
 I am much honoured.

LORD BONVILE.
 You cannot but deserve more
 By the title of her brother.

LACY.
 Another couple!

MISTRESS BONAVENT.
 Master Fairfield and my cousin are contracted.

MISTRESS CAROL.
 'Tis time, I think; sister I'll shortly call you.

JULIETTA.
 I ever wished it.

FAIRFIELD.
 Frank Trier is melancholy. – How hast though sped?

TRIER.
 No, no, I am very merry.

JULIETTA.
 Our banns, sir, are forbidden.

FAIRFIELD.
 On what terms?

LACY.
 My lord, you meet but a coarse entertainment.

How chance the music speaks not? Shall we dance?

Enter Venture and Rider.

VENTURE.
'Rivers of hell, I come!'

RIDER.
'Charon, thy oar
Is needless.' – Save you, gallants!

VENTURE.
'I will swim unto thy shore.' Art not thou Hero?

MISTRESS CAROL.
But you are not Leander, if you be
Not drowned in the Hellespont.

VENTURE.
I told thee 'I would drown myself a hundred times a day.'

MISTRESS CAROL.
Your letter did.

VENTURE.
Ah ha!

MISTRESS CAROL.
It was a devilish good one.

VENTURE.
Then I am come
To tickle the 'confines of Elysium.' –
My lord, – I invite you to my wedding, and all this good
company.

LORD BONVILE.
I am glad your shoulder is recovered;
When is the day?

VENTURE.
Do thou set the time.

MISTRESS CAROL.
After to-morrow, name it
This gentleman and I
Shall be married in the morning, and you know
We must have a time to dine, and dance to bed.

VENTURE.
Married?

FAIRFIELD.
Yes, you may be a guest, sir, and be welcome.

VENTURE.
I am bobbed again!
I'll bob for no more eels; let her take her course.

LACY.
Oh for some willow garlands!

Recorders sound within.
*Enter Page, followed by Bonavent in another disguise, with willow
garlands in his hand.*

LORD BONVILE.
This is my boy; how now, sirrah?

PAGE.
My lord, I am employed in a device.
Room for the melancholy wight,
Some do call him willow knight,
Who this pains hath undertaken,
To find out lovers are forsaken,
Whose heads, because but little witted,
Shall with garlands straight be fitted.
Speak, who are tost on Cupid's billows,
And receive the crown of willows,
This way, that way, round about,

Bonavent goes round the company with the garlands.

Keep your heads from breaking out.

LACY.
This is excellent! Nay, nay, gentlemen,
You must obey the ceremony.

VENTURE.
He took measure of my head.

RIDER.
And mine.

TRIER.
It must be my fate too.

Bonavent puts a garland on Trier's head.

VENTURE.
Now we be three.

BONAVENT.
And if you please to try, I do not think
But this would fit you excellently.

LACY.
Mine!
What does he mean?

MISTRESS BONAVENT.
I prithee, Master Lacy, try for once;
Nay, he has some conceit.

LACY.
For thy sake, I'll do any thing; what now?

Bonavent puts a garland on Lacy's head.

BONAVENT.
You are now a mess of willow – gentlemen –
And now, my lord, (*Throws off his disguise.*) – I'll presume to bid
you welcome.

Mistress Bonavent takes Lord Bonvile aside.

FAIRFIELD.
Is not this the gentleman you made dance?

LACY.
My new acquaintance! where's thy beard?

BONAVENT.
I left it at the barber's; it grew rank,
And he has reaped it.

LACY.
Here, take thy toy again

BONAVENT (*takes off the garland*).
It shall not need.

LORD BONVILE.
You tell me wonders, lady; is this gentleman
Your husband?

LACY *and* MISTRESS CAROL.
How! her husband, my lord?

BONAVENT.
Yes, indeed, lady; if you please you may
Call me your kinsman: seven year and misfortune,
I confess, had much disguised me, but I was,
And by degrees may prove again, her husband.

MISTRESS BONAVENT.
After a tedious absence, supposed death,
Arrived to make me happy.

VENTURE.
This is rare!

BONAVENT.
My lord, and gentlemen,
You are no less welcome than before. – Master Lacy,
Droop not.

LORD BONVILE.
This turn was above all expectation,
And full of wonder; I congratulate
Your mutual happiness.

VENTURE.
All of a brotherhood!

LACY.
Master Bonavent! on my conscience it is he?
Did fortune owe me this?

MISTRESS CAROL.
A thousand welcomes.

MISTRESS BONAVENT.
Equal joys to thee and Master Fairfield.

LORD BONVILE.
Nay, then, you but obey the ceremony.

LACY.
I was not ripe for such a blessing; take her,
And with an honest heart I wish you joys.
Welcome to life again! I see a providence
In this, and I obey it.

VENTURE.
In such good company 'twould never grieve
A man to wear the willow.

BONAVENT.
You have but changed
Your host, whose heart proclaims a general welcome.

MISTRESS BONAVENT.
He was discovered to me in the Park,
Though I concealed it.

BONAVENT.
Every circumstance
Of my absence, after supper we'll discourse of.
I will not doubt your lordship means to honor us.

LORD BONVILE.
I'll be your guest, and drink a jovial health
To your new marriage, and the joys of your
Expected bride; hereafter you may do
As much for me. – Fair lady, will you write
Me in your thoughts? if I desire to be
A servant to your virtue, will you not
Frown on me then?

JULIETTA.
> Never in noble ways;
> No virgin shall more honour you.

LORD BONVILE.
> By thy cure
> I am now myself, yet dare call nothing mine,
> Till I be perfect blest in being thine.

Exeunt.